A HISTORY OF WILTSHIRE

De Vaux College, Salisbury

THE DARWEN COUNTY HISTORY SERIES

A History of Wiltshire

BRUCE WATKIN

Cartography and Illustrations by
Jacqueline McCain
and Tom Murrow

PHILLIMORE

1989

Published by
PHILLIMORE & CO. LTD.
Shopwyke Hall, Chichester, Sussex

ISBN 0 85033 692 9

Printed and bound in Great Britain by
BIDDLES LTD.
Guildford, Surrey

Contents

Chapter		Page
	List of Maps	6
	List of Figures	6
	List of Plates	7
	Introduction	9
I	Ancient Wiltshire	13
II	Romano-British Wiltshire	21
III	Anglo-Saxon Wiltshire	30
IV	Under Norman Kings	38
V	The Late Middle Ages	49
VI	Tudor Wiltshire	60
VII	Stuart Wiltshire: Discord and Rebellion	71
VIII	Georgian Wiltshire	81
IX	The Agricultural 'Revelation' and the New Poor Law	91
X	More Revolutions	99
XI	Modern Wiltshire	113
	For Further Study	124
	Index	125

List of Figures

1. Stones in the great circle at Avebury, 1722 12
2. The Wansdyke above Calston, 1720 32
3. Old Salisbury in 1722 42
4. The Domesday Book entry for the borough of Malmesbury   43
5. Salisbury, from John Speed's atlas, 1610 51
6. Parliamentary inclosure 85
7. Address to the labourers of Wiltshire during the Swing Riots, 1830 94
8. Snap, a 20th-century deserted village 117

List of Maps

1. Wiltshire – Physical 10
2. Neolithic Wiltshire 15
3. Iron Age Tribes and Forts 22
4. Romano-British Wiltshire 25
5. Anglo-Saxon Wiltshire 34
6. Lands and Forests 40
7. Medieval Castles and Boroughs 56
8. Monastic Houses 64
9. Civil War 75
10. Travel – 17th Century 79
11. Georgian Houses and Parks 89
12. Wiltshire Workhouses and Poor-Law Unions 97
13. Turnpike Roads 1700-1800 and Stage Coach Routes 1790-98 102
14. Canals and Railways 103
15. Large Estates in 1873 108
16. Parliamentary Representation 110
17. Wartime 114
18. Modern Wiltshire 122

List of Plates

1. The Avenue, Avebury .... *between pages* 16/17
2. Stonehenge 16/17
3. Lynchets near Mere 16/17
4. Wansdyke from the air 16/17
5. The Bratton White Horse 16/17
6. Saxon chapel, Malmesbury 16/17
7. St Lawrence's Chapel, Bradford on Avon 16/17
8. Malmesbury Abbey, Romanesque sculptures 16/17
9. Malmesbury Abbey, Romanesque doorway 16/17
10. St John's church, Devizes .... *between pages* 48/49
11. Mere church and Priest House 48/49
12. Ludgershall Castle 48/49
13. The Market Cross, Malmesbury 48/49
14. The High Street, Lacock 48/49
15. The North Gate, Salisbury Cathedral Close 48/49
16. Salisbury Cathedral 48/49
17. Westwood church and manor house 48/49
18. Trowbridge stone 'lock up', 1758 .... 48/49
19. Great Chalfield (colour) .... *between pages* 64/65
20. Lake House (colour) 64/65
21. Malmesbury Abbey 64/65
22. Lacock Abbey 64/65
23. Corsham Court 64/65
24. Longleat 64/65
25. Holy Trinity, Easton Royal 64/65
26. Wardour Old Castle 64/65
27. Gateway, Fonthill Gifford 64/65
28. The Old Meeting House, Horningsham ..... *between pages* 80/81
29. Town Hall, Wootton Bassett 80/81
30. Goddard Memorial, Ogbourne St Andrew 80/81
31. Matrons' College, Salisbury 80/81
32. The Parade, Trowbridge 80/81
33. Melksham Spa 80/81
34. Stourton, St Peter's church (colour) 80/81
35. Castle Combe (colour) 80/81
36. The Palladian Bridge, Wilton House, 1737 ... *between pages* 96/97
37. Bowood House 96/97
38. Pythouse 96/97

39. Marlborough College 96/97
40. Amesbury Abbey 96/97
41. Horse-engine house, Horningsham 96/97
42. Model Farm, Quidhampton 96/97
43. George Ford, the Stonehenge shepherd 96/97
44. Semington Hospital ....,... 96/97
45. Tollhouse, Warminster .... *between pages* 112/113
46. Caen Hill locks, Devizes 112/113
47. The Engine House, Swindon 112/113
48. Abbey Mills, Bradford on Avon 112/113
49. Prospect Square, Westbury 112/113
50. Marlborough Town Hall 112/113
51. Avon Mill, Malmesbury 112/113
52. Windmill Hill Business Park, Swindon 112/113

Acknowledgements

The courtesy of the following for permission to publish illustrations is gratefully acknowledged by the author: Frank Rodgers (nos. 2 and 21); Ashmolean Museum, Oxford (no. 4); Roger Pizzey (nos. 5, 6, 8, 9, 12, 13, 26, 38, 49 and 51); John Davies (no. 16); Michael Blackman (no. 20); Wiltshire Archaeological and Natural History Society (no. 22); Derek Mee (nos. 39 and 50); and Dennis Stephenson, A.R.P.S. (no. 34).

Introduction

The county of Wiltshire is roughly rectangular, about thirty miles broad and fifty miles from north to south. It is unique in southern England in having neither direct access to the sea nor common border with the 'Great Wen' of Greater London. It has comparatively little manufacturing or extractive industry today, though its former cloth industry was renowned until its demise in the 1980s, just as were the great railway works at Swindon up to 1987. It was once one of the most heavily populated counties in the country and is now one of the least. In 1971, before the 1974 local government reforms destroyed so many of the historic counties, it was seventeenth in size but thirty-first in total population, while the density of the population was lower than any neighbour, less than half of that of Gloucestershire and Hampshire and less than a quarter of that of non-metropolitan Surrey.

John Aubrey (1626-97), author of Antiquities of Wiltshire *and* Brief Lives, *born at Easton Piercy*

It has long been called the county of 'Chalk and Cheese', notably by the 17th-century gossip John Aubrey who tried to explain the social differences between the people of the extensive chalk downs of the south and east and those of the narrower clay vales of the north and west. 'In the dirty claey country', he says, 'they feed chiefly on milke meates which cooles their brains too much and hurts their inventions. These circumstances make them Melancholy, contemplative and malicious . . . they are generally more apt to be Fanatiques'. On the chalk, however, which occupies two-thirds of the county 'tis all upon Tillage, or Shepherds, and hard labour, their flesh is hard, thier bodies strong; being weary after their hard labour they have not leisure to reade, and contemplate Religion'. While there have been continued differences in the history of north and south, Aubrey's division, like his sociology, is too simple. There is a belt of 'corn-brash' across the clay vales of the north and a fringe of Cotswold limestone along the northern border and there are sandy fringes, still covered with forest, in the south-west and south-east corners. Building stone is limited but a splendid limestone is worked near Box and a sandier limestone was worked for centuries at Chilmark between the downs of the south. Stone from the latter was used for the medieval cathedrals of Old and New Salisbury and as far away as Rochester, long before the virtues of the similar Portland stone were made known by Christopher Wren, who was born at East Knoyle. Other less valuable stones have been worked elsewhere, such as the attractive russet-coloured stone of the Sandy Lane area, the forest 'marble' and slates of the Cotswolds fringe, and the 'burr-stones' of the

Sir Richard Colt Hoare, Bt. (1758-1838), author of History of Modern Wiltshire *(1822-44) and* Ancient History of North and South Wiltshire *(1812-21)*

9

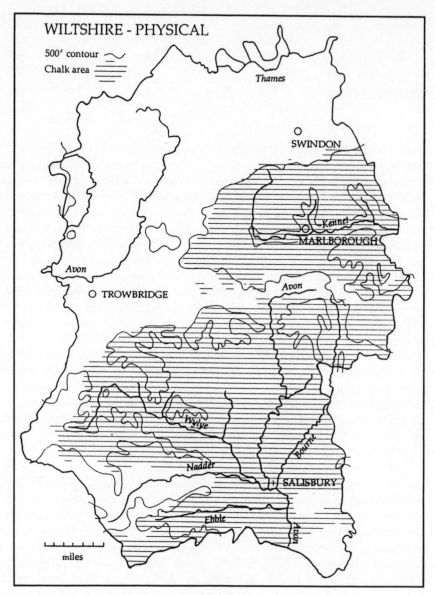

WILTSHIRE - PHYSICAL

500' contour
Chalk area

Thames

○ SWINDON

Kennet

MARLBOROUGH

Avon

○ TROWBRIDGE

Avon

Wylye

Bourne

Nadder

SALISBURY

Ebble

Avon

miles

Map 1.

Devizes and Warminster areas, but over the greater part of the county, the chalk lands, there was no good stone save the scattered blocks of sandstone 'sarsens', used for the prehistoric circles at Avebury and Stonehenge. This led to the extensive use of thatch, not only to cover

10

houses built of scarce timber but to protect house and walls built of chalk, though panels of flint were commonly used as facing material.

The county has no natural boundaries though in earlier times extensive forests separated it from its neighbours on the east, north and west. It has always been open to the south and it is up the southern, Salisbury, Avon that invasion and settlement have come.

Steeple Ashton church

A peice of the great circle. or Alien at the South Entrance into the temple at Abury Aug. 1722.

Abury

Fig. 1. Stones in the great circle at Avebury, drawn in 1722 by William Stukeley. From his *Stonehenge, a Temple restor'd to the British Druids* (1740).

I Ancient Wiltshire

Twenty thousand years ago Wiltshire was an almost blank sheet of snow and frozen soil above the bones of its native rocks, a legacy of the last great Ice Age which brought glaciers near its northern edge and permanent frost over the south. A warmer phase started some ten thousand years later, melting the ice and causing frost-shattered rock to flow into the valleys, but with succeeding centuries stabilisation of the land enabled soil to reform and forests to colonise it. First came birch trees, then pine and lastly mixtures of oak and elm, lime and alder, which filled the clay-covered valleys with dense forest and covered the thinner soils on the chalk hills with more open woodland.

England was still joined to the mainland of Europe as so much of the ocean waters were still locked up in the Polar ice-caps, and nomadic groups of hunters from the mainland traversed the Wiltshire area for thousands of years before making any regular settlements. Evidence of their temporary camps has been found, usually in the river valleys, in the form of hand axes and arrowheads but little else. The chilly climate discouraged settlement before about 6000 B.C., when continuously rising temperatures had melted much of the Polar ice and the ocean had flooded the Straits of Dover. Immigration became more difficult, but it is from this period that the first traces of settlement have been found, at Downton in the south and at Cherhill in the north of the county. Neither migrants nor early settlers were farmers, they were hunter-gatherers, but by 5000 B.C. they were already clearing considerable areas of forest. Some of this was accidental, the result of uncontrolled spread of their camp fires, but they were also learning to burn selectively, recognising that this would improve the grazing inside the forest and so attract more game.

Clearance of forest reached such a pitch that in another thousand years, about 4000 B.C., it had reached an ecological turning-point known as the 'Elm Decline' beyond which elm ceased to be one of the major self-perpetuating species. By this time, however, new immigrants of a Mediterranean type had introduced the first cereal seeds, the first domesticated cattle and new tools to cultivate the cleared areas and grow crops. These people are called Neolithic, meaning of the New Stone Age. Farming, hunting and fishing now overlapped but most Wiltshire settlers concentrated on farming, extending the forest clearance, cultivating, with primitive one-stick ploughs, the thin chalk soils of the downland and introducing cows and sheep to its simple landscapes.

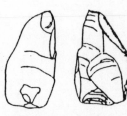

Mesolithic graver found at Christian Malford

13

Neolithic macehead of Great Langdale Stone, found at Aldbourne, 1956

The main areas of early Neolithic settlement must be judged from burials. In Wessex they were all on the chalk, three wholly inside modern Wiltshire, one straddling the Dorset border and another in southern Dorset. Those in Wiltshire were: **i**, on the Marlborough Downs, **ii**, on the western edge of Salisbury Plain, **iii**, on the Plain west of the Avon, and **iv**, in Cranborne Chase. The overall number of people is thought to have been very small, for a few tens of families could have cleared the whole of Salisbury Plain in a thousand years. They grew both wheat and barley, roughly in proportions of nine to one, and introduced domesticated cattle, sheep, pigs, goats and dogs. They also hunted the remaining wild cattle, deer, pigs, horses and even brown bear.

Their cultural and tribal centres seem to have been those curious enclosures with interrupted ditches which archaeologists used to call 'causewayed camps'. These were evidently not for the defence of their users and their exact functions are still disputed, but it seems likely that they were used for tribal gatherings, certain unknown ceremonial functions and the exchange of goods. The type site, which has also given its name to a distinctive early pottery, is that first recognised at Windmill Hill, north of Avebury. Its ditch encloses 21 acres and it was probably the central place for a group of settlers on the Marlborough Downs. Others were at Knap Hill on the north side of the Vale of Pewsey, at Robin Hood's Ball north of Stonehenge, which may have been the centre for the eastern Salisbury Plain group, and at Whitesheet Hill north of Mere, which was only five acres in extent and probably served the group in western Salisbury Plain. Another similar enclosure has been found at Rybury near All Cannings.

Aubrey Burl has suggested a link between the creation of these enclosures and a dramatic drop in activity in southern England when, between 3100 and 2850 B.C., some centuries of drier weather combined with probable overgrazing had impoverished both soil and settlers. These enclosures may then have been built by the more powerful groups of settlers as status symbols, on the edge of their territories, to warn off or overawe 'foreigners'.

These settlers developed trade with other areas, importing clay from Cornwall and also greenstone axes, and they started the first industrial projects in the county: the axe factory at flint mines at Easton Down near Salisbury and other flint mines at Durrington. But more interestingly they developed before 3000 B.C. a unique monumental treatment for the burial of their important dead. It involved the making of mortuary enclosures in which their bodies were laid out, and the erection of giant tombs known as long barrows. These had a chamber of wood or stone, usually at the eastern end, in which the dried skeletons of up to fifty bodies could be set; tailing back from this chamber was a long earthen mound. The best known of these barrows are at West and East Kennet,

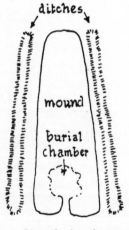

Plan of a long barrow

14

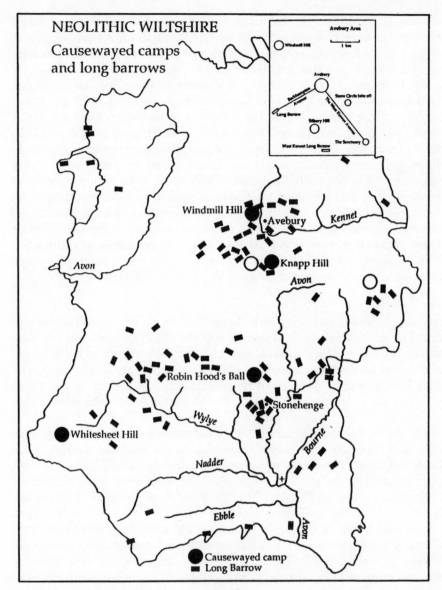

Avebury Area

1 km

Windmill Hill

Avebury

Stone Circle (site of)

Long Barrow

Silbury Hill

The Sanctuary

West Kennet Long Barrow

Windmill Hill

•Avebury

Kennet

Knapp Hill

Avon

Avon

Robin Hood's Ball

Stonehenge

Wylye

Bourne

Whitesheet Hill

Nadder

Ebble

Avon

● Causewayed camp
■ Long Barrow

Map 2.

which are some three hundred and forty feet long, and there is one at Tilshead 390 feet long. Wiltshire shows the highest concentration of such monuments, about one third of the known long barrows in the country. At a later date, probably five hundred years on, further ceremonial earthworks were constructed, sometimes elaborated with circles

15

of stone, and it is thought that those at Avebury and Stonehenge replaced the older centres at Windmill Hill and at Robin Hood's Ball. The most famous of such works and the best-known in the world is Stonehenge, but the largest and much older is that at Avebury.

They are now called 'henge' monuments and named, by a jocular back-formation, from the name given to Stonehenge, which meant hanging stones; the name is confusing because archaeologists have applied it to all prehistoric circular enclosures with an outer bank and inner ditch, places for meeting and not defence, irrespective of the presence of stones. They have been found all over the British Isles, but those with stones only west of a line, which includes Wiltshire, from Bournemouth to Scarborough. The following have been identified within the county area: Avebury, Durrington Walls, Marden, Stonehenge and Woodhenge; other prehistoric circles with or without stones have been identified at Fargo plantation, west of Stonehenge, Coneybury Hill to its south-east, Winterbourne Bassett and Sutton Veny, while other suspected rings have been wholly or partly destroyed by time and farming.

The Avebury area

Avebury is less known than Stonehenge but its history should be related first for, as Richard Colt Hoare of Stourhead, Wiltshire's busiest historian and antiquary, has said, 'it is the supposed parent of Stonehenge and the most ancient, as well as the most interesting relict which our island can produce'. John Aubrey took his king, Charles II, to see it and was even more enthusiastic, saying 'it did as much excell Stonehenge as a Cathedral does a parish church'.

The Avebury area had long been dominated by the circle on Windmill Hill and here has been found evidence of the trade in pottery from Cornwall, from the Cotswolds and from the Thames Valley, as well as fragments of oolitic limestone and red sandstone from Somerset, Oxfordshire slate, and Forest Marble from the Cotswolds. And on the brows of surrounding hills a number of long barrows of extravagant length and height were made in this period of active trade. But there followed a period when forests increased and grasses encroached on former ploughed fields. Sometime about 2900 B.C. a new kind of mortuary was developed when a round hut was erected for this purpose, on Overton Hill where it is crossed by the ancient Ridgeway about three miles from Windmill Hill and one mile from Avebury. It is now known as 'the Sanctuary' and has a complicated history which makes it seem likely that it may also have been a ceremonial circle, though without the ditch that marks the so-called 'henge' monuments.

In this same period, and again only a mile from Avebury, the largest prehistoric mound in Europe was built. This is Silbury Hill, a gigantic pyramid of chalk blocks laced with turves, 130 feet (39 metres) high and covering 5½ acres (2¼ hectares). In spite of repeated excavations, no sign of any burial has been found in the pyramid nor any other obvious reason

Silbury Hill

1. The 'Avenue', Avebury, looking south towards the 'Sanctuary'.

2. Stonehenge.

3. Prehistoric lynchets (cultivation terraces) at Chetcombe Bottom, near Mere.

4. Wansdyke from the air, 1933.

5. The Bratton White Horse, said to have been cut originally to commemorate Alfred's victory over the Vikings at Edington, was recut and reversed in the 18th century. An Iron Age fort lies above it, the ditch and rampart visible on the skyline to the right of the horse.

6. The Saxon chapel outside the West Gate at Malmesbury.

7. The late-Saxon church of St Lawrence, Bradford on Avon, 'rediscovered' in 1856. Possibly a rebuilding of the church constructed by St Aldhelm in 705, it had been used as a school and cottage.

8. Sculptures of six apostles and an angel in the south porch of Malmesbury Abbey, dating from the late 12th century.

9. Malmesbury Abbey, Romanesque doorway at the southern entrance.

for its construction. About the same time the early henge monuments at Durrington, Stonehenge and Marden were being started but involving only a ditch and bank with perhaps a single stone at the centre, and in the case of Stonehenge with a ring of pits which were almost immediately filled in.

The first of the important stone circles was not started for perhaps another hundred and fifty years, when one of sarsen stones from the surrounding downs was erected at Avebury. This was connected to the Sanctuary site by an avenue of more sarsens and by another avenue running to a now-unknown objective to its south-west. It should perhaps be said here that 'sarsens' or 'sarsen' stones originally meant simply 'foreign' stones, but the term is now confined to those great sandstone boulders found stranded on the chalk downs after a few million years of erosion. A few might once have been found on Salisbury Plain, but almost all have come from within the Marlborough Downs. Study of the Avebury avenues shows that by now descendants of the early settlers had been joined by a different people, or at least people with different customs, who are known as Beaker Folk because they buried their dead with a ceremonial beaker, and these people helped in the building of the avenues. They helped too in the building of a second ring of stones at Avebury just north of the first circle. Finally both circles were encircled by a massive bank and ditch, over a quarter of a mile in diameter, and the inner side of the ditch was lined with 100 sarsens larger than any used before and weighing up to fifty tons each.

The complex of multiple stone rings at Avebury, the lengthy stone avenues, the complicated mortuary chamber on Overton Hill and the Silbury Hill pyramid were all completed several hundred years before any great changes were made to the simple bank and ditch at Stonehenge. Fashions in upper-class burial changed and long barrows were abandoned. The bone chamber in the great West Kennet long barrow was walled in about 2250 B.C. and the important dead were now given their own private graves, usually in a round barrow, a mound about sixty feet in diameter. The barrows were still set prominently in the landscape, but often in straight lines as on the Ridgeway, north of the Overton 'sanctuary', and at Winterbourne Stoke near Stonehenge.

Bronze Age beaker, Beaker Folk

The Stonehenge area

In spite of the lack of change in the ring itself, the area around Stonehenge seems to have been of great importance, to judge by the great number of burial mounds that were made close to and around it. By about 2200 B.C. some of the Beaker Folk, descendants of those who helped at Avebury, had become masters of Salisbury Plain and the Stonehenge area within it. They now dominated the cross-roads of busy trade routes from east, west, south and north-east which brought copper and gold from Ireland and battle-axes of 'blue stone' (spotted dolerite) from Pembrokeshire to exchange for the products of continental Europe and

Ceremonial beaker, Beaker Folk

17

Bronze Age hut

eastern England. It is likely that these people, with their knowledge of Irish circles and their experience at Avebury, decided on the addition of a stone circle inside the simple bank and ditch at Stonehenge. For this they used not any stones still left on Salisbury Plain, nor the plentiful boulders of the Marlborough Downs, but boulders of 'blue stone' from north Pembrokeshire. They therefore brought in some eighty stones weighing about four tons each which had originated 135 miles away and, we presume, been brought by sledge and raft across the Bristol Channel, up the Bristol Avon and across land to the Salisbury Avon. We do not know why these stones were chosen, though their cultural importance as a source of battle-axes was well-known, and it has been suggested that they may have been used elsewhere on the Plain before being brought here. Certainly one other blue stone was used in Bowl's Barrow near Heytesbury several hundred years before this assembly at Stonehenge.

In addition to this ring another more massive stone was brought here, the so-called 'Altar Stone', which was 16 feet long and came from south Pembrokeshire. An avenue of ditches and banks was cut in the chalk north-eastward from the single (N.E.) entrance to the henge, and later extended first east, and then south-east toward the River Avon; it probably marked the route taken by these important stones. The making of the blue-stone circle was interrupted, however, when only two-thirds was complete. There seems to have been a revolution, for signs of the Beaker Folk almost disappear from the Plain though there is evidence of their culture continuing elsewhere. The new leaders of Salisbury Plain, perhaps also leaders of the Wessex area in view of their command of the old trade routes, were decorated with bronze daggers, and gold and amber ornaments, and they banished the blue stones and started to rebuild Stonehenge, using the massive sarsen stones, in a form that the world recognises today.

In this, five trilithons (two upright stones with another across the top) were set up in a horseshoe plan open to the north-east, that is toward the Avenue and the rising sun at midsummer, using sarsens weighing over fifty tons each. The horseshoe was encircled with smaller stones, still weighing over twenty tons each, with stone lintels. All the stones were dragged twenty miles from the Marlborough Downs and shaped. The standing stones were cut away to leave projecting pegs at the top while the lintels were given corresponding sockets underneath to fit the pegs and, finally, the lintels were carefully pared to make a neat butt-joint with their neighbours. These laborious tasks involved the techniques of carpentry, to which the builders must have been accustomed, and were largely wasted on these massive stones.

The organisers of this unique building grew rich on the international trade across Britain, particularly from the export of Irish copper to Europe, and not only commanded the obedience and patience of the

18

skilled workers who built Stonehenge but also that of a few jewellers of such exquisite ornaments that the comparatively short period of their output has been called 'The Wessex Culture'. Their products have been found in a number of the principal graves within sight of Stonehenge, notably of a man at Bush Barrow on Normanton Down who was buried with two bronze daggers, a bronze axe and a gold belt-fastener and, more exceptionally, in that of a woman in the 'Golden Barrow' at Upton Lovell a few miles to the west, who was buried with gold ornaments of great beauty and delicacy, and an amber necklace derived from Baltic Sea trade. Twists in the history of the monument continued for, following completion of the horseshoe and the outer ring, it was decided to return the blue stones and a large number of holes were prepared for them on the outside of the sarsen circle. This plan was abandoned, but the stones were eventually re-used, some in a smaller circle inside the sarsen circle, 19 in a horseshoe inside the trilithons of the sarsen horseshoe, and one near the centre of the henge. A number of carvings and 'boats of the dead' were cut in the sarsens but no further alterations were made to the general disposition of the complex, save that hundreds of years after the major changes and near the end of its long ceremonial life, the Avenue, as already mentioned, was extended towards the river.

The detailed functions of this elaborate monument, built over some one thousand years, will never be known, but it is likely that almost all those, whether religious or astronomical, that have been attributed to it are, in whole or part, correct. It is only surprising that, during its lengthy development and when burial and other ceremonies were radically changing, the monument itself was not abandoned. Nevertheless it was probably a ruin by 500 B.C. when the festivals of the new Iron Age and Celtic immigrants on the Plain paid more respect to sunsets than to the sunrise which had obsessed their predecessors. It is therefore ironic that the ruins are so often associated today with the Celtic priests known as Druids who would have treated it with scorn and probably abhorrence.

The end of the 'Wessex Culture'
The 'Wessex Culture' did not long survive the construction of the complex stone circles. Its place was taken by people with noses closer to grindstones, with less respect for the dead, less respect for this ancient monument and more interest in expanding and improving their farming.

What had happened? Copper and other important metals had been found in the Alps, which supplied the continental market, and in North Wales, which supplied those nearer home, and the new trade routes by-passed Wiltshire. The new populations had almost abandoned hunting and were now concentrating on cattle-rearing for which they made lengthy ranch boundaries, the larger leaving great banks across the inter-valley ridges. Indigenous and immigrant populations were expanding and causing land division so that many of the great ranches were divided by further boundaries running from the stream-side meadows to

Ornaments of amber and glass, and bronze dagger, excavated by William Cunnington from a barrow north of Stonehenge

19

the chalk hill-tops. Many of these form the basis of parish boundaries in the chalk country today. The immigrant population was associated with a tidal wave of population movements westwards from modern Germany and Holland which made iron-working common and Celtic languages almost universal in southern Britain until after the departure of the Roman legions eight or nine hundred years later.

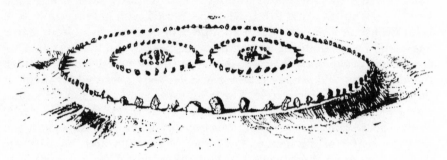

A reconstruction of the stone circles at Avebury

II Romano-British Wiltshire

The Iron Age

In the succeeding Iron Age, so-called because iron-working had become widespread and common, Wiltshire had lost its early advantages. It was now only one of many areas of easily-cleared and farmed land, the magnetism of its early monuments had evaporated or been replaced by revulsion, and it was no longer an important cross-roads of major trading routes. Yet continental products and influences still reached it from the south by way of the port at Hengistbury Head (now in Dorset) and to a lesser extent up the Thames valley from east-coast ports.

There was an increase of population and increasing conflict between different sections of this population. From about 400 B.C. a large number of extensive hill forts were built. Some of these were on or adjoined earlier ceremonial sites, like that on Whitesheet Hill near Mere, and some were enlargements of late-Bronze-Age forts like that at Yarnbury, 15 miles to the east, but many were on new sites like that at Bury Wood near Colerne, or Scratchbury and Battlebury which were only a mile apart on the north side of the Wylye valley. There were also many smaller defensive earthworks, but the major forts, which could soon be found from Sussex to the Severn estuary, had certain similarities. They all had multiple fortifications of two or three banks and ditches and they were extensively modernised from time to time. These large forts are now seen as 'capitals' of small regions covering, in Wiltshire at least, about forty square miles of downland. Few have been excavated (the most thoroughly explored is that at Danebury across the Hampshire border) but it is likely that most were occupied by numerous families, particularly towards the end of the pre-Roman era, and indicated rising insecurity.

'Celtic dispersal'

By the second century there had been considerable infiltration (immigration may be too strong a word) from the European mainland, part of a great 'Celtic dispersal' which reached England largely from the mouths of the Rhine. These people were called 'Belgic' by their neighbours in the Roman empire but, in Wiltshire at least, they showed little homogeneity or unity. Thus there was a division by the end of the pre-Christian era between the peoples of north-east and south-west Wiltshire. The division varied but ran roughly along the line of the Salisbury Avon and Wylye rivers. It was marked by differences in pottery styles and,

Iron Age ard, a primitive plough

21

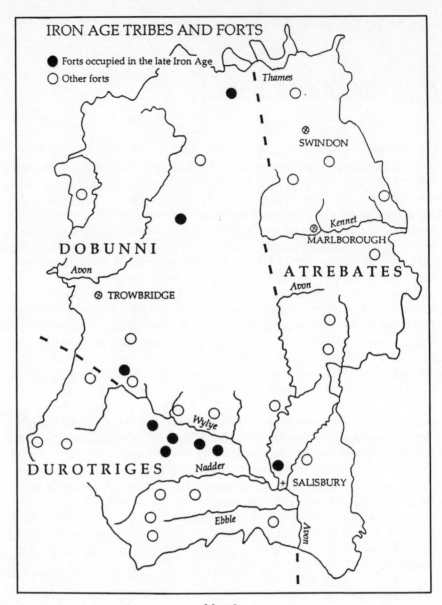

Map 3.

later, in the design of coinage, as well as by the creation of a threatening series of forts facing each other across the Wylye valley.

While these new forts show considerable complexity in their fortification and some in their internal planning (as far as it can be deduced),

22

domestic settlement away from these 'capitals' was as far as ever from sophistication. Careful excavation of a contemporary farm at Tollard Royal illustrates a common pattern. Here the farmhouse consisted of a simple round hut 14 feet in diameter; nearby were four granaries above ground and 33 pits, some of which were suitable for more grain storage. They were all within a kite-shaped enclosure less than a quarter of an acre in extent and surrounded by a three-foot-deep ditch. The large space between the buildings left plenty of room for the penning of the farm's stock. Similar development of native farms has been found at Little Woodbury and at Boscombe Down on Salisbury Plain. While this may be the norm, some more complex farmsteads have been found such as those along the Great Ridge at Barford, Hanging Langford, Ebsbury (near Great Wishford) and Stockton, which have interlocking enclosures, themselves enclosed within a wide and substantial ditch; at Stockton the farmstead is 100 acres in extent. Most of these survived well into the era of the Roman conquest.

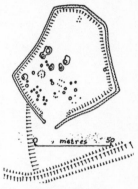

Iron Age farm, Berwick

Roman interference

By the time of the exploratory invasions of the country by Julius Caesar in 55 and 54 B.C., silver coins were well distributed in Wiltshire. Both the Durotriges, as the people of Dorset and south-west Wiltshire were now known to the Romans, and the Atrebates of Hampshire and north-east Wiltshire copied Roman forms. After these invasions, when the power of Rome had been felt, the Atrebates minted coins showing the name of their leader as Commius, a Gaul who had had dealings with Julius.

Commius had taken a pro-Roman stance and been used by Julius as an intermediary with other British leaders, but he later supported the revolt of Vercingetorix against the Romans in central France and after the latter's defeat in 51 B.C. was lucky to escape back to Britain. He was succeeded in about 25 B.C. by his son Tincommius, who like most of the leaders in Britain was now opposed to making treaties with Romans, in part because they now thought themselves safe from invasion. But ten years later it was significant that the Atrebatic coinage was now modelled on the Roman denarius (the basis of our old penny) and minted by a skilled die-cutter who was probably an immigrant from the Roman Empire. It is deduced from this that the Atrebates were more friendly to Romans and may even already have had a treaty of friendship with them. Whatever the date, change there was and this was due to pressure on them from the Durotriges on their south-western flank and from the still more aggressive Catuvellauni, who were expanding from their Essex base up the Thames valley.

Tincommius was succeeded by Eppillus and then Verica, both of whom adopted the Roman title of *rex*, but, opposed by an anti-Roman party, Verica fled to Rome. The Romans had long been considering the conquest of Britain and Verica's arrival may have given Claudius the

Coin of Eppillus, King of the Atrebates

23

pretext of legitimacy he sought, in defending a client king, for the conquest and exploitation of Britain, which was known as a refuge of enemies and was thought to be rich in valuable minerals. Claudius's well-planned and successful invasion in A.D. 43 led to the submission of his chief opponents (and enemies of the Atrebates), the Catuvellauni, at Colchester. Verica was then restored as king of the Atrebates although he was almost immediately replaced by a younger and more Romanised leader, Cogidubnus.

Use was now made of the Atrebatic kingdom, which included a safe harbour at Chichester, as base for the conquest of the still hostile Durotriges and other clans in the west of England. It was from here that the general Vespasian, later emperor, took the Second Legion on its show of strength across the south-west, probably by way of Old Salisbury, to smash opponents defending the Durotrigean fortresses of Hod Hill and Maiden Castle (Dorset) before marching on into the territory of another hostile clan, the Dumnonii, to establish a military base at Exeter by A.D. 47.

At the same time the Roman army was used to secure and then work the silver and lead mines of the Mendips. By about A.D. 49 pig-lead was already being exported to the continent across Wiltshire by a new road via the Great Ridge and Old Salisbury to the channel ports at Chichester and Southampton.

Roman occupation

Another important and still largely surviving road, known as the Fosse Way, was built to connect bases on the western frontier zone from Bath to Lincoln. It ran along the Cotswolds on the north-western edge of the county and through a new administrative centre established at Cirencester (Gloucs.). Other roads were made across the county from Cirencester to Salisbury and the south coast, to Silchester (Hants), another important centre of the Atrebates, and from Silchester south-westerly through Salisbury (where it crossed both the 'lead route' and the road south from Cirencester) to run on to Dorchester, the new administrative centre for the Durotriges. One other important new road was made, from Silchester westerly to Bath by way of Silbury Hill, and this forms part of the modern Bath Road. By the A.D. 60s southern England had been pacified and the process of civilian Romanisation, which was already advanced in east Wiltshire among the Atrebates, was under way among the other peoples by education and example. The army was now pulled out for further service in the conquest of Wales and the North. The new city of Cirencester, just beyond the northern tip of modern Wiltshire, was promoted into a regional capital from which south-western Britain was governed for most of the Roman occupation. More local administration was conducted from the sub-regional capital at Silchester, but there was no home rule of, or delegation to, the modern county area.

Roman military martingale

24

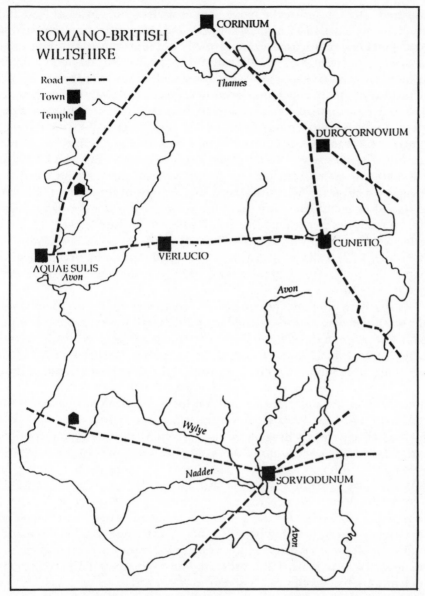

ROMANO-BRITISH
WILTSHIRE

Road - - -
Town ■
Temple ⬠

CORINIUM

Thames

DUROCORNOVIUM

AQUAE SULIS
Avon

VERLUCIO

CUNETIO

Avon

Wylye

Nadder

SORVIODUNUM

Avon

Map 4.

The effects of invasion and occupation on the county were not as dramatic as on many other parts of Britain and apart from giving many peasants and slaves another change of masters, tended to sterilise the status quo for much of four centuries. In spite of a network of good roads which greatly improved the movement of such commodities as lead and grain to the ports and also of soldiers and administrators, few of the road junctions stimulated urban growth to the extent that might have been expected. Only at Mildenhall did a small town, named Cunetio, succeed as a market and service centre, and it was even enlarged and refortified in the troubled fourth century. There were smaller settlements at Sandy Lane, called Verlucio, and at Wanborough, called Durocorno-vium, on the road to Cirencester. The last became a small manufacturing centre and was given a *'mansio'*, that is a posting house to receive travelling administrators and other imperial guests. But at Old Salis-bury, adjoining the Iron Age fort where five roads met and provided the biggest junction in Wiltshire, there is little sign of much development. It should be mentioned here that Old Salisbury was not normally called 'Old Sarum' until perhaps the 18th century. The Roman name for the place was Sorviodunum. The first mention in the Anglo-Saxon Chronicle (for A.D. 552) calls it Searobyrg. The medieval abbreviation for its name was 'Sar', and when misguided pedants wanted to Latinise it, they made of it *'Sarum'*.

As southern England became more prosperous under its pacification the wealthier British traders and farmers followed the example of Roman administrators in building 'villas', country houses usually headquarters of an estate, which were of increasing complexity and of luxury. Their sites have been found concentrated around the Romanised towns of Bath and Cirencester from which they spread into north-west Wiltshire. More are scattered around Cunetio and Verlucio, in the Avon valley below Salisbury and near West Dean on the south-east border. But there is a marked absence of them from most of the chalk downland and particu-larly in the huge area south of the Vale of Pewsey, west of the Salisbury Avon and south to Cranborne Chase on the present Dorset border. In this extensive area only two villa sites have been found, at Netheravon and at Pit Meads near Sutton Veny. From this absence it has been reasonably deduced, though not proved, that the area was taken from its former owners, whether hostile or not, and treated as a huge imperial estate supplying corn direct to the army or for export overseas, so having no need of a local market and providing no opportunity for local farmers and traders to become rich enough to build villas.

Most of the population, however, whether on chalk or elsewhere, still lived in isolated houses or tiny hamlets, although a settlement at Hamshill Ditches near Groveley Wood covered some forty acres. Other, smaller, villages in a nuclear form are also found on the Great Ridge near to the 'lead route' and some in a more linear form on the downs further north, e.g. at Chisenbury Warren and West Overton, but none had the formal layout of a Roman town or fort. Nevertheless, under a stable administration agricultural production increased for the first three centuries of occupation, and the small square fields of the 'Celtic'

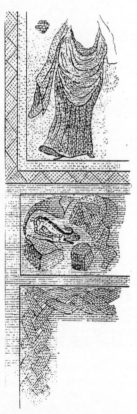

Roman mosaics from the villa at Pit Meads

26

farmers were replaced by larger rectangular fields worked by heavier and stronger ploughs, which were able to tackle heavier land. The population rose with this agricultural growth.

In respect of local customs the Roman administrators were tolerant, at least where these did not conflict with strategic aims or inhibit tax-collection. They readily absorbed local gods into official worship. Pagan temples were built at Nettleton Shrub on the Fosse Way, which became an important religious centre, and a less important shrine on Cold Kitchen Hill, near Maiden Bradley and the 'lead road', which had existed for centuries before the Roman Conquest, was given a more permanent temple. But few other pagan religious centres are known although all the towns must have had their temples.

The temple at Nettleton Shrub

Britain, with the rest of the Empire, became officially Christian under Constantine I, a little after A.D. 313, but there is little evidence of Christian worship of these times in Wiltshire, though a temple-like structure at a villa in Littlecote Park may have had a Christian function. Wiltshire did not have the long tradition of Christian worship that was found further west in Somerset. From the third century onwards there was an extension of both arable land and of sheep rearing so that both the corn and wool exports from Wiltshire grew. But there was a decline in the prosperity of the smaller towns due first to a concentration of administrative and manufacturing functions, and then of markets, in larger centres. Increasing taxation to support the Roman occupation seems also to have had a deleterious effect but the population of Wiltshire and much of Britain fell during most of the fourth century due to a variety of causes.

The decline of Roman Britain

More serious instability was created by affairs on the continent where leadership of the Empire was frequently disputed. Much of the Roman army in Britain was taken to the continent, from which it did not return, to fight for various pretenders to the imperial crown. In this period of weakness there was a joint attack on Britain by Franks, Picts, Scots, Irish and Dutch, known as the 'Barbarian Conspiracy', in A.D. 367. This spread chaos over much of the country north of the Thames and encouraged separatism. The Bokerly Dyke on the Dorset border was rebuilt to block access from Wiltshire as though it was from Wiltshire that pillage and massacre would come, while a line of villas from Bath across to Verlucio seem to have been burnt about the same time, possibly from a raid up the Bristol Channel. But, apart from the contemporaneous destruction of villas in northern Wiltshire (which may not have been connected, but only coincidence) and some increasing emigration from the countryside, it is difficult to see the effects of these fourth-century troubles. Luckily stability was restored in 369 when Valentinian (emperor 364-75) sent his general, Theodosius, to Britain, for Theodosius restored order in the province and reorganised its frontiers. In line with

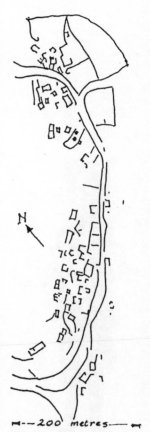

← 200 metres →

Sketch plan of the Romano-British settlement at Chisenbury

27

his policy of consolidation, the town of Cunetio was reinforced. Its walls were largely rebuilt with an improved dry-stone core between mortared-stone faces some 16 feet wide at the base. These were extended on the west side of the town to enclose a larger area, and projecting bastions to take artillery were added as well as a wide, flat-bottomed ditch to keep attackers at a distance. Here, at Cunetio, has been found early evidence of the stationing of troops with German tastes in decoration, if not actually of German origin, who had presumably been brought by Theodosius. Certainly the practice of employing German mercenaries was common by now and many of them may have been settled upon lands in Wiltshire abandoned after the barbarian incursions.

But in spite of reorganisations and refortifications stability was soon threatened again by continental disputes. Near the end of the fourth century there were three separate occasions on which local commanders took armies from Britain to fight for the imperial throne. Few troops returned, so that the effect of the removal of so many able-bodied men from the countryside, particularly a sparsely populated area like late-Roman Wiltshire, was severe. Even more serious was the reduction in the amount of Roman coinage brought in to pay the troops. After the third continental expedition, by Constantine III (emperor 407-11), imperial officials were thrown out by the British, who were being pillaged by unruly mercenaries while the country was being fragmented amongst local tyrants. The 'Dark Ages' were beginning.

It was at the turn of the century that the succeeding emperor, Honorius, told the city regions in Britain that they must be responsible for their own defence, but even though it was not recognised at the time Britain was already lost for ever from the Roman Empire. One Briton, who called himself Vortigern, a British name which means 'high king', appears to have led the anti-Roman party in Britain and yet to have maintained the province intact against attacks by Picts and Irish, then the most dangerous of its enemies, by employing Saxon mercenaries and rewarding them with land in Kent. They appear to have been used to guard the east coast and inland as far as Dorchester (Oxon.). But he was himself upset by a revolt of the mercenaries and was replaced by Ambrosius, one of the last patrician Roman Britons and leader of the pro-Roman party.

Sometime between A.D. 446 and 454 Ambrosius addressed a last appeal to Rome for military assistance. It is called 'The Groans of the Britons' for he complained that 'the barbarians drive us into the sea; the sea drives us back to the barbarians'. It went unanswered. But there was no immediate collapse in the Romano-British way of life, which to the barbarians must have seemed one of unparalleled luxury and one which many of them were anxious to adopt, for even Bede, although writing much later, admits to periods of peace and prosperity. There was certainly a slow decline which followed from the loss of the Roman

Bronze figure of Mercury found at Southbroom, Devizes

28

soldiers, however. First the loss of coinage, then the loss of markets, then the decay of the highways, which became unsafe for travellers. Roman coins ceased to be imported about A.D. 400 and by 430 were hardly in use in the province.

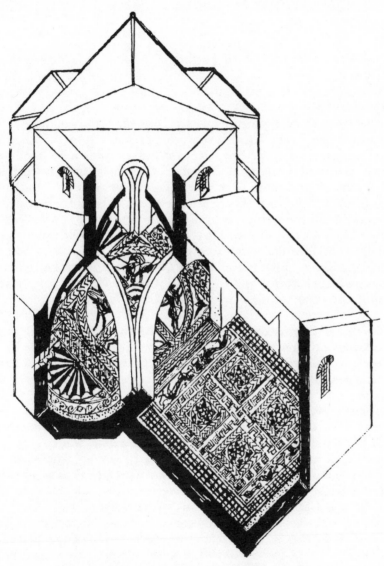

An isometric reconstruction of the Roman villa at Littlecote

III Anglo-Saxon Wiltshire

The grave of an Anglo-Saxon warrior at Petersfinger. His sword and spear are to his left, shield on his right shoulder and belt and knife at his waist

The three centuries from the departure of the Roman legions at the end of the fourth century to the accession of Ine as king of Wessex at the end of the seventh are often called the 'Dark Ages'. This is not just because the economy of the country started to revert to that of the Iron Age but more because our evidence for reconstructing the history of those centuries is scarce and weak. There is confusing archaeological evidence from the excavation of many early pagan Saxon graves; but it is extraordinarily difficult to date the timing of their parent settlements even when such sites are found, and more so to determine the newcomers' relationship to the Britons of the area. There are few traces of early Saxon buildings and worst of all the written record is scant and wildly prejudiced.

The earliest written record is that of Gildas, the first British historian, a Romanised Christian monk who died about A.D. 572 and had seen some of the Saxon immigration. In his *De Excidio Britonum* he viewed the pagans with such horror and so vehemently criticised the petty kings of Britain for inviting for their defence the 'fierce Saxons of ever execrable memory, admitted into the island like so many wolves into the fold' that he cannot be trusted to have given a balanced account. He tells us of the battle of Badon, though without mentioning Arthur, where Britons defeated marauding Saxons, but writing from the Welsh borders he had no knowledge of peaceful settlement in eastern and south-eastern England.

Our next source is another West-Country monk (or monks) called Nennius, who collected fragments of British history in the ninth century. These tell us of the battle of Badon where Arthur, leader (*'dux'*) not king of the Britons, won one of a series of 12 famous battles, the last being at Camlann where he was killed. Badon, which does seem to have marked a pause in Saxon movement westward, is now dated to about A.D. 495 and Camlann (probably in northern Britain) to 515.

The next record of Saxon activity comes from the Anglo-Saxon Chronicle. The Anglo-Saxon Chronicle is a record in Old English, and the first history in any native North-European tongue, of events from the birth of Christ to the end of the reign of King Stephen in 1154. It appears to have started as a church calendar of Easter tables with additional notes on special events, and to have been put in ordered form first by King Alfred of Wessex in the 890s. It has a strong Anglo-Saxon and Wessex, perhaps even Wiltshire, bias and entries up to A.D. 449 are very brief. That for 449 records that Hengist and Horsa, leaders of

30

Jutes, were employed by Vortigern, but while it is known from the archaeological record that Saxons had long settled in the Thames Valley it is not for nearly another century that the Chronicle records a direct incursion into Wiltshire territory.

The creation of Wessex
In 519, says the Chronicle, Cerdic and Cynric 'obtained of the West Saxons the kingdom', which was based probably on the Roman sub-regional capital of Winchester. They conquered the area around Southampton Water and the Isle of Wight and then moved inland, defeating a British force at Charford on the Hampshire border. They defeated another British force at Old Salisbury in 552 but probably controlled southern and eastern Wiltshire before then, as many pagan burials predating the sixth century have been found around Salisbury.

In 556 Cynric went on to defeat another British force at Barbury Castle near Swindon. Four years later his son Ceawlin 'succeeded to the kingdom of Wessex', as the Chronicle calls it for the first time, and he extended the kingdom eastward into Surrey and then in 577 northwards, defeating a British force at Dyrham, a few miles north-west of the modern Wiltshire border, in a battle which enabled him to take the decayed Roman towns of Gloucester, Cirencester and Bath. The numbers involved in these battles were probably small, for Cerdic and Cynric came to England to carve out a kingdom with only five ships and perhaps two hundred and fifty followers, and even as late as the seventh century, in King Ine's famous law code, 'up to seven men were thieves, from seven to thirty-five a band, and above three dozen an army'. The battle was decisive, however, for it effectively cut off the Britons of the West Country from those of the Midlands and Wales, and prevented forever any concerted effort to drive out the more aggressive Saxons.

Ceawlin attempted to extend his power further north but, whether from meeting hostility from Saxon neighbours to the north and east or solely from a dynastic dispute, he suffered a defeat at Adam's Grave, a prominent long barrow on the north side of the Vale of Pewsey, and was driven from his kingdom. This last battle was close to the longest ancient earthwork in the county, the linear 'Wansdyke', i.e. the dyke of Woden, chief god of the pagan Saxons. It runs 12 miles across east-central Wiltshire on the north downland side of the Vale of Pewsey, from Morgan's Hill eastwards to the edge of Savernake Forest two miles south of Marlborough. It has an impressive ditch and bank some ninety feet wide overall, with a few causeway crossings. In spite of a number of excavations it can only be dated loosely to between A.D. 450 and 600. It was long assumed to be a defence built by Romanised Britons, led perhaps by Arthur, against Saxons of the Upper Thames valley, but it now seems more likely that it was built by Ceawlin to anticipate an attack by northern Saxons. Its significance was short-lived and present

The Wansdyke

Fig. 2. The Wansdyke just above Calston, 20 May 1720, drawn by William Stukeley. From his *Stonehenge, a Temple restor'd to the British Druids* (1740).

parish boundaries, sometimes based on pre-Saxon estate limits, pay it no respect.

Leadership of the Saxon kingdoms then passed for many generations to those to the north, and it was under pressure from the kings of Mercia that Wessex was introduced to Christianity. St Augustine had been sent to England by the Pope in 597 to convert the country. His mission was successful and Christianity spread rapidly among the Saxons, though some, like Redwald of East Anglia, worshipped pagan gods simultaneously. In 635 Birinus, a Benedictine monk from Rome supported by the Mercians, was given the newly created see of Dorchester, Oxfordshire, and there baptised Cynegils of the house of Cerdic, now king of Wessex.

The son and grandson of Cynegils started a new period of Wessex expansion westward by defeating Britons at Exeter, and taking control of Devon, Somerset and east Cornwall as well as absorbing Dorset, so that Wiltshire was now the heartland of the kingdom. King Ine, the best-known of the early rulers, succeeded in 688. Apart from making the first laws for good government since the departure of Romans, laying down the blood-price for killing Saxons and Welshmen, as his British subjects were now known, Ine encouraged learning and the Church. He refounded the ancient monastery at Glastonbury and put in charge his talented kinsman Aldhelm, who had done so much to improve the abbey at Malmesbury. In 706 the Pope permitted Ine to divide the large see of Winchester, which had been founded in 662, into two, a new see being created round Sherborne for Wessex west of Selwood; Ine appointed Aldhelm as its first bishop. He went on to secure the submission to Wessex of London, Essex and Kent, and he defeated a Mercian invasion at the second battle of Adam's Grave in 715.

Rivalry and disputes with the powerful Mercians continued for most of the eighth century; the marriage in 787 of the king of Wessex, Beorhtric, to the daughter of Offa, the greatest king of Mercia, was an attempt to heal the rift. But rivalry with Mercia continued in spite of the dynastic marriage, and a raid from Mercia across the Thames at Kempford in 802 was defeated by the 'Wilsaetan', i.e. the men of the Wilton or Wylye area, as the Wiltshire Saxons were called for the first time. After a further defeat at Ellandun near Swindon, in 825, the Mercians accepted the leadership of Wessex, as did the Northumbrians: all were now facing the considerable external menace of Viking raids.

The impact of the Vikings

Viking raids on the Wessex coast had begun as early as 787 but for long remained unorganised. The raiders gave little thought to settlement and had little effect on an inland county like Wiltshire. But in the next century, the ninth, increasing and more powerful raids were made across both central and southern Britain from which the raiders retreated to ships on the east coast as winter came on. They became a still bigger menace when they started settling in less-densely populated parts of East Anglia.

Sometime before the end of the ninth century Wessex was organised into shires, each under the leadership of an 'ealdorman' as the king's representative, and each shire had its 'fyrd', a force of men subject to compulsory military service, at least within their own county. Alfred, of the house of Cerdic, was now in charge of an army for the defence of Wessex made up of these fyrds and dealt well enough with most of the hit-and-run Viking raids. In 878, however, when he had succeeded his elder brother to the throne, he was caught out by a Danish force led by Guthrum, who now controlled the old East Anglian kingdom. Alfred had chased Guthrum's army from Wareham and Exeter and forced them to retreat into the Mercian town of Gloucester before he retired to spend

Part of the cross shaft at Codford St Peter, with the 'Dancing Man'

33

ANGLO-SAXON WILTSHIRE

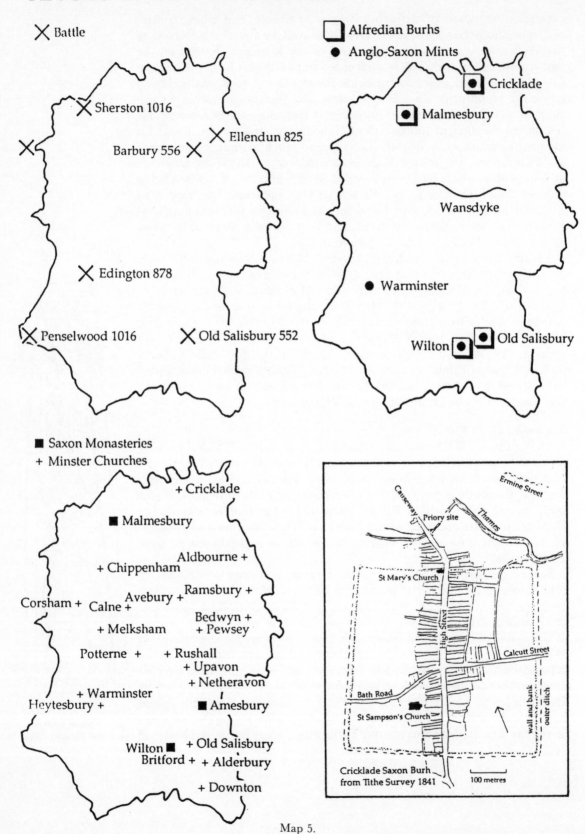

✗ Battle

✗ Sherston 1016

✗ Barbury 556   ✗ Ellendun 825

✗ Edington 878

✗ Penselwood 1016   ✗ Old Salisbury 552

☐ Alfredian Burhs
● Anglo-Saxon Mints

◼ Cricklade

◼ Malmesbury

Wansdyke

● Warminster

Wilton ◼   ◼ Old Salisbury

◼ Saxon Monasteries
+ Minster Churches

+ Cricklade

◼ Malmesbury

Aldbourne +

+ Chippenham

Ramsbury +

Corsham +   Avebury +

Calne +

Bedwyn +

+ Melksham   + Pewsey

Potterne +   + Rushall

+ Upavon

+ Netheravon

+ Warminster

Heytesbury +   ◼ Amesbury

Wilton ◼   + Old Salisbury

Britford +   + Alderbury

+ Downton

Ermine Street

Causeway   Priory site   Thames

St Mary's Church

High Street

Calcutt Street

Bath Road

St Sampson's Church

wall and bank
outer ditch

Cricklade Saxon Burh
from Tithe Survey 1841

100 metres

Map 5.

a quiet Christmas at Chippenham. But Guthrum, instead of going back to Suffolk, 'went secretly in midwinter after Twelfth Night to Chippenham and rode over Wessex and occupied it' to quote the Chronicle. Alfred escaped with a few men through Selwood to the Somerset marshes and prepared to reorganise his scattered forces. After Easter he called on the fyrds of Somerset, Wiltshire and east Hampshire to meet him at 'Ecgbrytesstan to the east of Selwood', probably the estate boundaries at Willoughby Hedge, near Mere. From there he went the following day to 'Iley Oak', the meeting place of a hundred near Longbridge, and the next to the edge of the downs at Edington near Westbury. Guthrum came out to meet this threat but was soundly beaten and after two weeks' siege in Chippenham, surrendered, swore to leave Wessex for good and to receive Christian baptism. The dispirited chalk figure of a horse below Bratton Camp is probably a recut (and reversed) version of an early memorial to the battle.

Edington was not the end of Alfred's troubles with Danes and he set about learning some lessons from them. First, he built a fleet to intercept Danish ships at sea and, second, he adopted the Danish system of forts and avoiding, where possible, pitched battles. In Wessex he made his forts into a network of small towns, no more than 40 miles apart, into which the local population could fly when threatened; these 'burhs' were planned as new towns with a commercial basis rather than as simple forts. Their fortifications consisted of a high bank surmounted by a heavy timber fence, surrounded by a ditch, their plan commonly being rectangular. Inside, building plots were laid out on a regular grid. Modern Cricklade still retains the layout of its Alfredian foundation. To ensure the upkeep of the burhs, special rates were levied on the surrounding population which were in proportion to the length of the defences in each case. Apart from Cricklade, burhs were established in Wiltshire at Malmesbury on the Avon-fringed spur where Aldhelm's abbey was now famous, at Wilton and at Chisbury, near Great Bedwyn. At Wilton the burh was commercially successful but it was difficult to defend, so in times of stress its administrators and moneyers would move to the older fort of Old Salisbury; thus the two places acted in tandem. Chisbury was perhaps the inverse of Wilton for it was a small fort of only 15 acres, intended more for the protection of the important royal estate of Bedwyn. It certainly never became a market town as did its companion Bedwyn.

The White Horse at Westbury as seen in 1772, said to commemorate the Battle of Edington, A.D. 878, but possibly a tribal symbol of the Atrebates, who controlled eastern Wiltshire before the Roman invasion. The chalk figure was enlarged and reversed in 1778

The Wiltshire burhs were given the right to mint their own coins, which helped to establish successful markets. The resultant stability in Wiltshire led to the development of other small market towns, such as Ramsbury, Bradford on Avon, Calne, Marlborough, Tilshead and Warminster. In 909 the first of these six was made the seat of a new bishopric, carved like Sherborne from the diocese of Winchester, to serve Wiltshire and Berkshire. It was as a consequence of these developments

Tenth-century coped gravestone of an early, unnamed bishop, Holy Cross, Ramsbury

that Maitland could say of Wiltshire at Domesday that it was 'quintes-sentially the county of small boroughs', and that later it had a dispropor-tionate number of seats in the king's parliament.

Alfred was the first English king to fight the Danes to a standstill, work that was continued by his son, daughter and grandson so that his great-grandson, Edgar, was able to receive the submission of both the Danish settlers and all the other English kingdoms and to be recognised as the first king of a united England at an elaborate coronation at Bath in 973. After them Saxon England, in the hands of weaker successors, fell under the increasing domination of the Danes until 1013 when Aethelred II, known as the 'Unready', had lost most of his kingdom outside traditional Wessex, and fled to Normandy before the attacks of an angry Sweyn, King of Denmark. Sweyn's followers had swept right across Wiltshire in 1010 and 1011 and previously burnt Wilton in a lightning raid as early as 1003. The tide was almost turned by Aethel-red's son Edmund 'Ironside', who defeated Sweyn's men at Penselwood and again at Sherston and was able to make peace with Sweyn's son Cnut, but on Edmund's mysterious death in the same year Wessex and the other kingdoms submitted to Cnut, who was now king of Denmark and Norway. Stability during Cnut's reign was followed by some anarchy under his sons and then by the ascent to the throne of Edward 'the Confessor', half-brother of Edmund.

Wiltshire was not ignored by the late Saxon kings in their new grandeur and in reigns from Athelstan, who was buried in Malmesbury Abbey in 939, to Cnut they paid more formal visits to Wiltshire than to any other shire.

Edward the Confessor's death in 1066 led to a dispute over the succession. The English councillors elected their fellow Harold, Earl of Wessex, in preference to Harold Hardrada, King of Norway, and to Duke William of Normandy who claimed the throne both as related to both Cnut and Edward and because (he said) he had been promised it by Harold of Wessex. The foreign claimants invaded England almost simultaneously; Harold of Wessex defeated Harold Hardrada in York-shire but was defeated and slain by the Normans near Hastings. Saxon and Wessex domination of England ended with him.

The Saxon legacy

Angel, St Lawrence's church, Bradford upon Avon

Wiltshire still has a strong Saxon legacy: so much of the landscape in the patterns of fields and woods, the siting of villages and small towns, as well, of course, as the name, shape and very existence of the shire. In terms of monuments and art there is little to see beyond the largest of all, the Wansdyke and the Saxon burhs – Cricklade in particular. A large number of churches were built though most were of timber and have either decayed or been totally rebuilt, but two small and almost complete Saxon churches have survived in stone. The best preserved is that of St Lawrence, at Bradford, which, while mainly of the tenth

36

century, is almost certainly successor to the one founded by St Aldhelm from Malmesbury in about 706. The other is a recent discovery at Malmesbury itself, a small chapel outside the West Gate, which had been used as a dwelling for some centuries. Of other church building only the tower at Netheravon shows unmistakable Saxon construction, but there are several excellent pieces of Saxon sculpture. These include the decorated arch at Britford, where Edward the Confessor heard of the Northumbrian rebellion in 1065, a unique cross-shaft at Codford St Peter carved with the figure of an ecstatic man holding an alder branch, which was considered pagan and subversive by Normans who buried it in a wall, and other cross-shafts at Colerne and Ramsbury. At Ramsbury are also two coped gravestones of Saxon bishops, for the church was a cathedral from 909 to 1058. At Knook is a tympanum carved with beasts in low-relief interlacing, rebuilt in a blocked south door, and at Inglesham is a tender relief of the Virgin and Child with the hand of God above. Of the beautifully decorated late-Saxon manuscripts of Malmesbury and Wilton Abbeys, few have survived. They were scattered at the Reformation and in the 17th century Aubrey's schoolmaster at Leigh Delamere used them for wrapping his books.

Tenth-century Virgin and Child, St John the Baptist, Inglesham. The church was restored in 1888-9 with the help of William Morris

Part of the Anglo-Saxon Chronicle entry for 878, recording the Battle of Edington

37

IV Under Norman Kings

Saxon thegn

With the death of Harold, last Earl of Wessex, William 'the Conqueror' did not receive the immediate surrender of the English which he had expected and therefore advanced with caution, making a wide sweep westward round London and threatening moves towards both Winchester and Highworth on the way. At Berkhamsted, where he had cut off the northern Saxon leaders from those still left in London, he received the surrender of London and the crown from Edgar, grandson of Edmund Ironside, who though still a boy had been elected king by the Londoners, and his bishops. The effects of this conquest are still disputed but while it can be seen as just another dynastic quarrel, it made more difference than a simple change of landlords, a takeover by five thousand newly-frenchified Norsemen. There were major changes.

First, there was more central control. The older freedom to hold land and elect earldormen who could elect their king was turned upside down, and the Norman '*nulle terre sans seigneur*' (no land without a master) was applied as meaning that all land was held directly or indirectly from the king. William took a great deal of land into his own hands, not only that of Edward the Confessor and his queen but also that of all the Saxon leaders who fought his invasion or subsequently rebelled against him.

An additional burden of military service, in the form of 'knight's service', was imposed over and above the former fyrd and other common obligations to the king. And a great number of castles, a Norman introduction, were built to maintain the security of the new government. Not long after the conquest William started translating military service in person into money payments, called 'scutage'; this money was used to hire increasing numbers of mercenaries in the succeeding 12th and 13th centuries and to build up near-permanent armies to fight in Scotland, Wales or France.

Norman knight

The church was reorganised, its sees and abbeys were filled with more able and better-educated priests, and most of the major churches were rebuilt in the 'Romanesque' style. Jurisdiction of religious matters was separated from that of lay ones. Few people now agree with the view (*c.*1930) of Sir John Fortescue, historian of the British Army, that 'England passed to her good fortune under the sway of a nation that could teach her to obey', but most probably share the view expressed in *1066 and All That* by Sellar and Yeatman's pupils that 'The Norman Conquest was a good thing as from this time onwards England stopped being conquered and was thus able to become top nation'.

Domesday Survey

While many of the English lands had been shared out by the king and his councillors among their adherents, they were ignorant of the country's resources and of how far these could support the new nobility. In 1085, therefore, when the king was at Gloucester, he 'held very deep speech with his wise men about the land, how it was held, and with what men' as the Anglo-Saxon Chronicle relates. An inquest was held in the following year to ascertain for each manor in the country, how much land was there, how many plough-teams, how many tenants and sub-tenants, villeins, cottagers, slaves, meadow, pasture, woodland and mills as well as its value at King Edward's death and 'now', i.e. in 1086.

The meaning of much of the information provided by this survey is obscure and the subject of argument. There were also plenty of disputes at the time such as that between Richard Poingiant of Alvediston, who claimed that he held land directly from King William, and the nunnery at Wilton, which claimed that he was their tenant. In addition the unit of survey was the 'manor' which was an estate and which cannot always be identified today but could include a village, hamlet, a single farmhouse, or all of them, separated sometimes by some miles, with the implication that its owner held it directly from King William or from a 'tenant-in-chief' who did. Nevertheless this survey, which was called a 'descriptio' in its own time and was only known as 'Domesday', a day of judgment, some ten years later, is hugely informative and is a document unique in European history. It showed that the county was, as it had been earlier and was to be down to the 20th century, one of large estates.

Estates

Of the estates, 53 were in excess of 20 hides and 10 were larger than 50 hides. The hide then varied in size from place to place – usually larger on the poorer soils – but it implied enough land to support a self-sufficient family, and was later standardised on Glastonbury Abbey estates as 120 acres. The largest holder of land in 1086 was, as to be expected, King William, who had taken not only the royal estates, which included the boroughs of Bedwyn, Calne, Tilshead and Warminster, but also the extensive personal estates of Edward's and Harold's families. His estates now covered nearly one fifth of the area of the county.

Next in size were those of four great ecclesiastics who had built up large estates by gift and purchase well before the Conquest: the Bishop of Salisbury (his see was of course at Old Salisbury not New), the Bishop of Winchester, the Abbot of Glastonbury and the Abbot of Malmesbury. The Salisbury estates were concentrated in three blocks, viz., at Ramsbury, a former seat of Wiltshire's bishops, in the Vale of Pewsey and around Salisbury itself. Those of the Bishop of Winchester were in a large block round Downton and a smaller block around the Knoyles. Of the total land in the county the two bishops held some seven per

The principal tenants-in-chief in Wiltshire, from Domesday Book

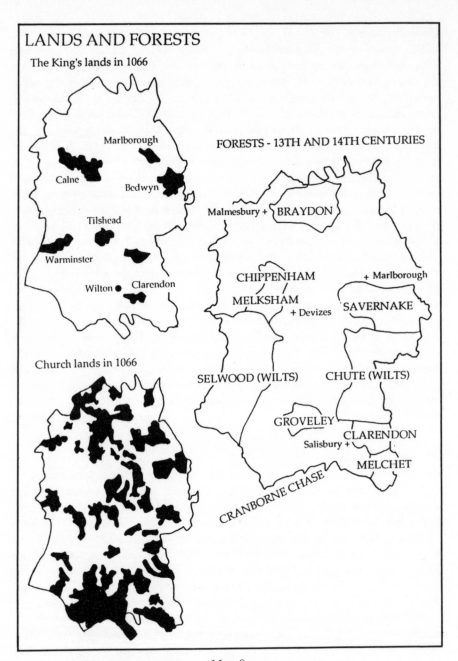

Map 6.

cent each, the Abbot of Glastonbury about six per cent and the Abbot of Malmesbury about five per cent.

Other churchmen also held land in Wiltshire. The Bishops of Bayeux, Coutances and Lisieux, William's friends or relations, were granted 16,

24 and 12 hides respectively, but in their personal not official capacities. Lands held by the Norman Abbot of Bec and the Canons of Lisieux, which had been granted to them before the Conquest, were not disturbed, but many church-owned lands were appropriated by newcomers who claimed that the previous holder had been their 'antecessor' and to hold it 'in chief', i.e. directly from William. The Church nevertheless counter-claimed, as is often recorded in the Domesday Book, that these lands 'could not be separated from the Church', as did the Abbot of Glastonbury at the Deverills and the Bishop of Winchester at Downton, Ham, Enford, Overton and Stockton.

Of the new tenants-in-chief only Edward, Earl of Salisbury, who was now Sheriff of Wiltshire in succession to the Confessor's sheriff (kept on for some years after the Conquest), had extensive holdings. His lands covered some five per cent of the county, but in line with William's policy were scattered in 42 pieces, none bigger than the manor of Wilcot which was taxed at $15\frac{1}{2}$ hides but had a 'new church, a very good house, a good vineyard' as the survey notes with evident envy. The Earl was rewarded for his service as the king's deputy in the county by receipt of all the fines for law-breaking as well as a large number of perquisites such as the annual tribute of 162 pigs, 1,600 eggs, 240 fleeces and so on, but he was also responsible for the collection of taxes from the county and could be mulcted from his own resources if these failed to meet the king's expectation or demand.

Castles
The Earl of Salisbury's seat was now at Old Salisbury where a stone keep was erected in the centre of the Iron Age fort and its remaining Saxon fortifications. The former population was removed and the whole of the fort's site was treated as the bailey to the new keep. Other castles were built at Ludgershall and Marlborough for the king, at Trowbridge for the de Bohuns following its loss by Odo, William's half-brother, at Devizes by the Bishop of Salisbury and minor fortifications were made at Ashton Keynes and perhaps also at Clack, Oaksey, Sherston and Great Somerford. These castles were concentrated in the north of the county but did not at any time match the taxing rash of new castles erected in the rest of the country. Nor was there in Wiltshire a Saxon revolt like that at Montacute in Somerset, provoked by the Count of Mortain building a castle on the sacred peak of Montacute in 1086. But the savage repression of such revolts there and elsewhere in the West, seems to have made a mark on south Wiltshire, simply by the passage of rapacious soldiers, and is indicated by the reduced value of manors in that area.

Population
The survey does not include all the population, or even all the heads of households, but nevertheless gives a fairly clear picture of its distri-

Dripstone moulding, Malmesbury Abbey

41

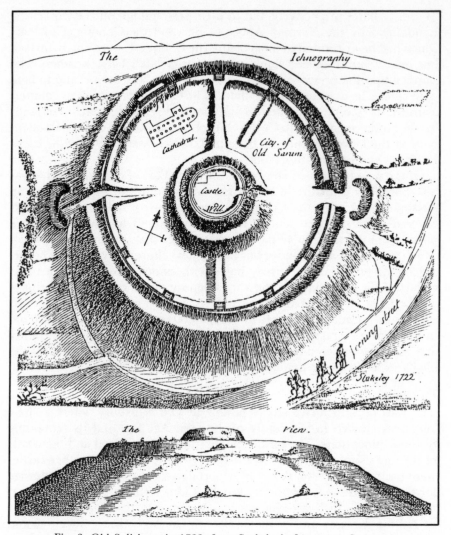

Fig. 3. Old Salisbury in 1722, from Stukeley's *Itinerarium Curiosum*.

bution. The major divisions are not so different from the position today and reflect the contrast between the Chalk Country and the Cheese Country which was noted by the antiquaries Leland in the 16th century and Aubrey in the seventeenth.

In the chalklands of the centre and south, population densities were high close to the Salisbury Avon and its tributaries. They were high in the rich Vale of Pewsey and along the Kennet east of Marlborough, while they were low on the north-west side of Salisbury Plain and to its west along the Great Ridge whose chalk upland is obscured by a layer of clay with flints. In the centre of the Plain however is a surprise. This is Tilshead, one of the late-Saxon boroughs, for here a large area of meadow and nine mills were recorded where there is today only a winter-flowing stream. The record of course refers to the whole manor, which may have included some land in the Vale to the north, while the water-table at Tilshead at that time was higher than it is today.

In the clay vales there were low densities in the north, in the extensive Bradon Forest on the cold Oxford Clay, but they were high on the mixed soils from Chippenham to Warminster and again in the Vale of Wardour in the south-west corner of the county. Population was low along its north-west border on the fringe of the Cotswolds, but the number of mills along the deep-cut streams there was high. On the Hampshire border, where there was an extensive forest fringe, later to be designated as the Royal Forests of Chute, Clarendon and Melchet, there was the lowest density of population in the county.

Information about the towns is scarce but 10 boroughs can be identified. Malmesbury is the only one given special mention, for it had a mint, 100 burgesses and a probable population of about five hundred. Four others, Bedwyn, Calne, Tilshead and Warminster, were, as already mentioned, parts of large royal manors. Tilshead, in the middle of Salisbury Plain, had already been important as a sheep and wool

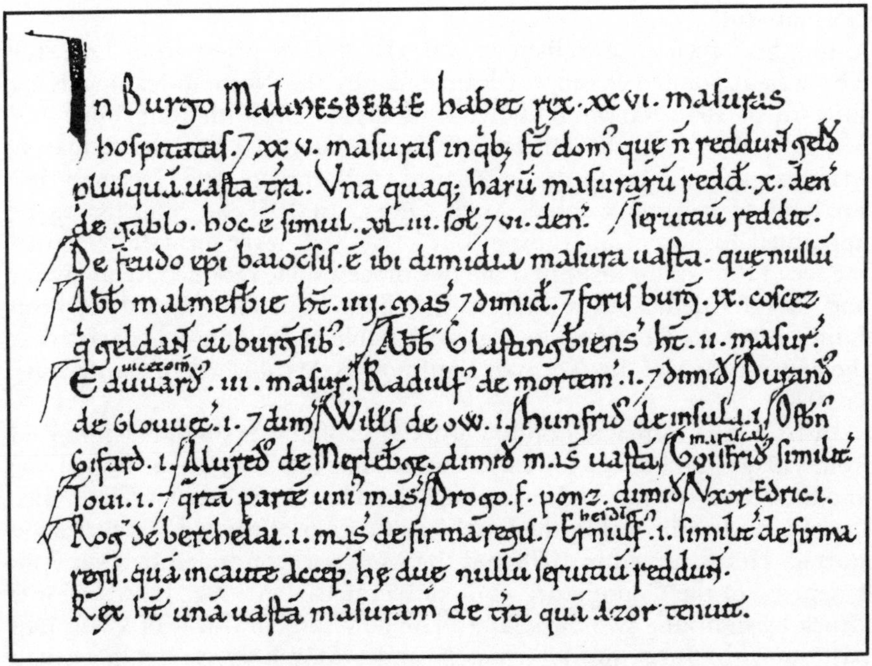
In Burgo MALMESBERIE habet rex .xxvi. masuras
hospitatas. 7 xxv. masuras in qb; st dom que n reddunt geld
plusquā uasta tra. Vna quaq; harū masurarū redd. x. den
de gablo. hoc ē simul. xl. iii. sol 7 vi. den. / seruitiū reddit.
De feudo epi baiocsis. ē ibi dimidia masura uasta. que nullū
Abb malmesbie ht. iiij. mas 7 dimid. 7 foris burg. ix. coscez
q geldant cū burgsib. / Abb Glastingbiens ht. ii. masur.
Eduuard uicecom. iii. masur. / Radulf de mortem. i. 7 dimid / Durand
de Glouuec. i. 7 dim / Wills de ow. i. / hunfrid de insula. i. / Osbn
Gifard. i. / Aluredus de Merlebge. dimid m.s uasta / Goisfrid marescal similit
Iovi. i. 7 qrta parte uni mas / Drogo. f. ponz. dimid / Vxor Edric. i.
Rog de berchelai. i. mas de firma regis. 7 Ernulf de heidin. i. similit de firma
regis. quā in cautē accep. he due nullū seruitiū reddunt.
Rex ht unā uastā masuram de tra qui Azor tenuit.

Fig. 4. The Domesday Book entry for the borough of Malmesbury.

A naughty nun, after L'image du monde, *a treatise on ecclesiastical law*

collecting centre in late Saxon times. Two others were centres of large ecclesiastical manors, Bradford on Avon of the Abbess of Shaftesbury and Old Salisbury of its bishop. Of the others Cricklade was one of the burhs founded by King Alfred, Marlborough adjoined a royal castle and Wilton was the early administrative centre of the county as well as being another of Alfred's burhs.

It may never be possible to estimate the population of the county – estimates for England as a whole vary widely – but the number of individuals recorded in the survey was 9,735, of whom 35 per cent were villeins, that is they were occupiers of family farms, and 16 per cent were serfs and virtually slaves. The number of serfs in Wiltshire as in most of Wessex was high, considerably higher than in eastern England, and it is thought that the Conquest had caused a considerable downgrading of the peasants there. The average population was about fifty persons to the square mile, like its neighbouring counties, even though three-fifths of its area was chalk downland occupied by sheep rather than humans. The county was ranked tenth of English counties in the number of persons actually recorded.

The Church

Following the building of the new castle at Old Salisbury, the latter's importance was increased by the transfer there of the Wiltshire see from Ramsbury. It affords a bizarre illustration of transition from Saxon to Norman rule.

The first Bishop of Salisbury was Herman, a priest from Lorraine who was appointed Bishop of Ramsbury by the Norman-leaning King Edward in 1045. Herman showed his discontent with Ramsbury and was offered instead the abbacy of Malmesbury. To this the monks of Malmesbury objected, the offer was withdrawn, and Herman left England to become a monk at St Omer. In 1058 he returned to be appointed Bishop of Sherborne, but as he had never formally resigned the see of Ramsbury he united the two dioceses. He retained royal favour and in 1065 dedicated a church at Wilton built for Edward's Queen Edith. After the Conquest he was acceptable to William and assisted at the consecration of the Norman Lanfranc as Archbishop of Canterbury in 1070.

In 1075 the Council of London ordered that all sees should be removed from villages and small towns to 'cities' and the joint see of Ramsbury and Sherborne was accordingly transferred to Old Salisbury. The building of a new cathedral in the north-west corner of the old fort was soon started. Herman died in 1078 and the work was continued by Osmund, a nephew of the Conqueror, who consecrated it in 1092. Its tower was struck by lightning two days later. The new cathedral was of a Norman pattern with three apsidal chapels and was relatively small, with a short choir and a nave of seven bays, only 173 feet long overall. It was

13th-century tiles from Clarendon Palace

almost doubled in size by Bishop Roger from 1125 to 1138, but even then it did not compare with the new churches at Winchester or Westminster.

Forests

Forests were of great importance to the Norman kings for their hunting if only as a reservoir for deer, as Oliver Rackham has suggested, but restrictions placed on cultivation and the former rights of common in order to protect this hunting, coupled with the extension of 'forest laws' to wide areas outside, caused considerable resentment. Florence of Worcester, writing after the hunting incident in which William II was killed in the New Forest in August 1100, evidently thought his death was a work of divine providence for he says 'At the bidding of King William the Elder the men were driven away, their houses thrown down, their churches destroyed and the land kept as an abiding place for the beasts of the chase, and thence it is believed was the cause of the mischance'. But such complaints, while not new, may well have been exaggerated. Royal Forests were not novel: Wulfgeat and Aluric, huntsmen of Edward the Confessor, were given land in Chippenham and Clarendon Forests respectively for their services, and William the Conqueror took over the woodlands and the customs of his predecessor. It is true that the Norman kings enforced their forest laws rigorously and then extended their application by arbitrary decrees to huge areas of land beyond the forest boundaries, but dispossession seems to have been rare. Only two hides on the Downton manor of the Bishops of Winchester were recorded as 'waste' from which 'men dwelling on them were driven on account of the King's forest'.

The forests were centred on the royal estates, those of the north and west on estates from Lydiard to Warminster and those of the east on properties from Bedwyn to Collingbourne, and they were generally on poor soils with few inhabitants. But the 'forests' were so greatly extended that by the 13th century nearly one third of the county was subject to their draconian provisions. Some favoured families became hereditary wardens such as the Esturmys for Savernake Forest and the Crokes for Chute Forest, who were descended from Norman huntsmen. But to tenants in and around the forest they provided constant grievances, made worse by the tyrannical and often corrupt conduct of foresters, who at Melksham for instance 'sold the king's wood to the great injury of the king and the countryside'.

The Norman kings mixed business with pleasure and made good use of the hunting lodges, particularly of Clarendon in the south-east corner of the county, into which a northerly extension of the Hampshire New Forest was created by the Conqueror and his son William Rufus. This included Clarendon Park, which was the largest medieval park in the country, five square miles in extent with an encircling deer fence some three miles in diameter. The park's lodge was enlarged by later kings, notably Henry II and Henry III, to cover six acres and become one of

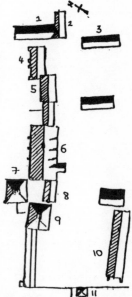

Clarendon Palace

1. *The Queen's Chambers*
2. *Chapel*
3. *Great Wine Cellar*
4. *'Antioch' Chamber*
5. *King's Chamber*
6. *Great Hall*
7. *Household Kitchen*
8. *Larder*
9. *King's Kitchen*
10. *Stables (?)*
11. *West Gate*

45

The 'Empress' Matilda, from the Devizes charter of 1141

the finest royal houses in England. The Constitution of Clarendon confirming the ancient customs of the kingdom and reaffirming the king's superiority over the Church on temporal matters, was issued here in 1156. It was unwillingly witnessed by Archbishop Thomas à Becket and led indirectly to his death. After Edward III's victory at Poitiers in 1356, King John of France was imprisoned here and in 1359 a great hall of Chilmark stone was added to the palace, 83 feet long and 51 feet wide. Nothing now remains but a short length of flint wall and a misleading Victorian inscription commemorating the Constitution.

Civil war

Wiltshire was to suffer considerably before the Constitution was signed, during the reign of the Conqueror's grandson, Stephen, last of the Norman kings, whose government alone seems to make nonsense of Sir John Fortescue's adage. Apologists for King Stephen can blame much on Roger, Bishop of Salisbury from 1107 to 1139, an impatient Norman priest who is said to have been chosen by Stephen's uncle Henry I because of the speed at which he could say mass. He became in turn Chancellor to Henry and Justiciar (king's deputy) to Stephen, though he had previously promised to support the succession of Henry's daughter Matilda. He was addicted to castle building, rebuilt the castle at Old Salisbury, built a new castle on parish boundaries at Devizes (hence the name of that town) and refortified Malmesbury in 1118. He was arrested by Stephen in 1139 for causing trouble, as well as for building unauthorised castles. His nephew the Bishop of Ely fled to his uncle's castle at Devizes, where he and Roger's mistress were besieged by Stephen who threatened to kill both Roger and Roger's son if they did not surrender. The castle was surrendered but Bishop Roger died soon after, it is said, from ill treatment when imprisoned.

Churchmen generally while deploring military pretensions in their bishops were outraged by their maltreatment and, on a wave of public indignation against Stephen, his cousin Matilda landed to claim the throne that had been promised her. There followed 13 years of anarchy and civil war, which raged between London, Oxford and Bristol across Wiltshire, so that the tale of the castles besieged, betrayed, recaptured and refortified reads more like a catalogue than an historical account. A castle at Cricklade which had been built without licence was taken and has since disappeared without trace, Devizes was taken and retaken five times, Downton (a castle of the Bishop of Winchester) was taken once, Malmesbury twice and Marlborough once, while Salisbury and Trowbridge castles resisted siege but Wilton, in spite of Stephen's new fortifications of 1143, surrendered. Peace was made eventually in which it was agreed that on Stephen's death he should be succeeded by Matilda's 'Plantagenet' son Henry.

The tax roll for the second year of Henry II's reign (1156) gives some indication of the devastation caused in Stephen's wars. Over one third

46

of Berkshire, nearly one third of Gloucestershire, about one quarter of Wiltshire and nearly a fifth of Somerset were described as 'waste'. There was physical recovery and a growth of population by the end of the century but this led to considerable inflation with rising prices and, relatively, falling wages. The large landlords, like the bishops of Winchester and the abbots of Glastonbury, took back more and more land into their own hands, insisted on all the customary labour services of their tenants and generally became more market-oriented and capitalist in their management. There was a considerable increase in sheep farming.

Local government

Stephen's wars had weakened the authority of the crown and decreased the importance of Winchester as the ancient capital and seat of the king's treasury. But they strengthened the position of the king's deputy in the county, the sheriff, the earliest and most important crown official outside the capital.

The office's title goes back to the original division of Wessex into shires. The sheriff was responsible not only for collecting the king's dues but for administering justice, keeping the peace and mustering troops. Under the later Norman kings the post became almost hereditary; the first Norman appointee in Wiltshire was Edward, Earl of Salisbury, and his son, three grandsons and a granddaughter, Ela, all became sheriffs. Following the death of Ela, who had married one of Henry II's many natural sons and founded Lacock Abbey, the office passed to less exalted officials of the court, like the Mauduits and Tregozes, and then to even smaller landholders. In matters of justice they slowly lost ground first to the king's travelling justices 'in eyre' (from the Latin '*itinere*' meaning on a journey) and then to the more local Justices of the Peace.

Below the county were the hundreds, administrative districts which were originally based on 100 family-farm units and in Wiltshire were all constituted by the tenth century, if not much earlier. Their courts met every four weeks to administer purely local matters, such as the apportionment of taxes.

Beneath these layers of government, the majority of the people lay under the tyranny of the manorial system. Nobles and knights were usually subordinate only to the king but others were subject to the courts of their respective lords of the manor. The 'Lord', a title which did not imply ennoblement, usually retained part of the land of the manor in his own hands, the 'demesne'. The rest was occupied by tenants or used for common or waste. Tenants were bound to the lord and paid 'rent' in the form of services, sowing, reaping, carting dung and so on. As time went on many such services were commuted to cash payments and demesnes rented out, but when demand for land rose landlords tried to take it back into their own hands and to re-impose labour services.

Thus in 1247 tenants of the Abbey of Bec at Brixton Deverill had to work three out of six working days for their lord throughout the year,

13th-century tiles from Clarendon Palace

the full six days for the lord at harvest time and to cart cheese forty miles to Southampton (for export to Normandy), wool thirty miles to the parent house at Ogbourne and corn ten miles to the market at Shaftesbury. In the same period tenants on the Glastonbury manor of Longbridge had to take the 'monks' cloth' 28 miles to the abbey whenever required. Manorial courts governed the management of commons and waste, the transfers of land, the rights of lord and tenants and escheats. The latter was the reversion to the lord of property where a tenant died without an adult heir. Heirs when old enough had to pay a fine to reclaim their inheritance. Escheats were not abolished until 1925. During the 12th and 13th centuries many such courts turned manorial dues into slavery from which villein tenants could only escape by running away and never returning (for they were considered the property of the lord) or joining the Church, for which they would still have to pay a fine to the lord.

Monuments
Wiltshire is not rich in Norman monuments. Only an outline marking the foundations of Osmund and Roger's cathedral on the hill-top of Old Salisbury is left, although much of the castle overlooking it survives. Devizes has the splendidly ornamented late-Norman church of St John, probably built for Bishop Roger, and Manningford Bruce, a complete village church built over the ruins of a Roman villa. The finest relic is probably at Malmesbury Abbey, already some centuries old by the Conquest, which retains in the portrayal of the Apostles over its south door the finest sculpture of its time in the country.

Norman window, St John's church, Devizes

48

10. St John's church, Devizes. The tower and chancel are Norman and the South or Beauchamp Chapel dates from the 15th century.

11. St Michael's church, Mere, and the 'Chantry House', a late-medieval priest's house.

12. Ludgershall Castle. Remains of the flint-built keep and extensive castle in use from the 11th to the 15th centuries.

13. The Market Cross, Malmesbury, built around 1500 'for poore folkes to stande dry when rayne commeth', said Leland.

14. The High Street, Lacock. The market place of a 'new town' of the early 13th century. Lacock got its charter in 1232.

15. The North Gate, Salisbury Cathedral Close, with the Matrons' College on the right. The town council's authority stopped at the gate.

16. Salisbury Cathedral, begun in 1220; the spire was added about 1334.

17. Westwood church and manor house. The house and church tower were built in the 15th century by Thomas Horton, a successful Bradford clothier.

18. Trowbridge stone 'lock-up' of 1758 adjoining the Town Bridge of 1777.

V The Late Middle Ages

Farming

The population of the county increased continuously from 1086 up to the time of the great plague in the mid-14th century, and this increased pressure on the land. There were more 'assarts', areas of woodland cleared and converted to arable land, and Edward I even sold parts of his Clarendon Forest during this period for the purpose, while Maiden Bradley Priory was granted leave to enclose parts of Selwood Forest on the opposite side of the county.

Improved management of much farmland was also undertaken by large landlords, especially by the great church landowners. It was largely inspired by a period of inflation in the early 13th century when prices rose and real wages fell, so that demesne farming became very profitable. Much capital was then sunk on the great estates in farm buildings, for example by the abbots of Malmesbury on their compact estate round that town and the bishops of Winchester at Downton, East Knoyle and Fonthill manors. The abbots of Malmesbury also carried out extensive reclamation in the late 13th century, improving the marshy land at Rowmarsh and Fowlswick and inclosing former common land for the protection and improvement of stock. On the Downton estates of the bishops of Winchester, that of Lacock owned by the abbey there, and on the estates of the abbots of Glastonbury, in the north and south of the county, particular instructions for the spreading of dung were introduced. On most estates it had now become 'customary', and therefore obligatory, for tenants to plough their lord's land three times a year instead of twice as formerly.

Monument to Sir Edward Cerne (died 1393), and Elyne, his wife, Draycott Cerne. The brass has been mutilated

Generally the manors of the chalk-stream areas adopted a two-field system, leaving fields uncultivated in alternate years, while much of the new arable fields on the heavy clay in the north, and also some of the new fields taken from old chalk pastures, were farmed under the more efficient three-field system which needed a fallow period only once in three years. Neither system was universal and the more primitive two-field system remained the more common for a century or so. An even cruder system was used in some areas, for example at Stoford on Wilton Abbey land, where tenants had to work 12 days each a year 'denchering' the demesne land. In this the soil was allowed to relapse into weeds and wild grasses before being ploughed, when the turves, after being turned to ash by slow burning in piles, were scattered over the ground. Following this, crops were grown until all the goodness was gone and

13th-century builders

49

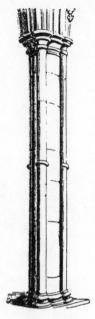

the process was repeated. (A modified system known as 'Burnbake' was practised on some downland until the 20th century and is commemorated in local field names.)

Most of Wiltshire's arable land was cultivated on the common-field system widespread in central England, in which the community of each manor worked huge unenclosed fields in strip allotments. Each occupier had a certain number of long narrow strips scattered about the manor's fields. Less commonly, meadow land was divided in the same manner. After harvest and in times of fallow, both arable and meadow were opened to common pasture by the community or, more strictly, by the lord and his tenants, who also had common pasturage of the 'waste', with rights to collect firewood, furze and turf. All these activities were controlled, theoretically in common, by those attending the manorial court.

It is not clear when this change to 'common fields' from the former individual fields of Celtic and Roman times took place, but it probably originated with late Saxon settlement. There is little documentary evidence of their existence in the county, or anywhere else, before the 13th century though they had doubtless existed for a long time before.

Column, Salisbury Cathedral, c.1250

New towns

Population was growing not only in country areas but also in the towns, and a number of established towns were extended and new towns were planted by the great landlords of the early 13th century so as to obtain revenue from their markets. The Bishop of Winchester did the former at Downton in 1208 and the latter at Hindon in 1219. Other examples, more usually large extensions to existing places like that at Downton rather than a wholly new settlement as epitomised by Hindon, are Sherston, Wootton Bassett (which obtained its charter in 1219), Old Swindon and Highworth in northern Wiltshire, and Lacock (charter of 1232), Heytesbury (charter 1214) and Warminster in the west.

Such places were distinguished by a rectangular grid of 'burgage' plots and a wide market-place. Not all were successful and both those of the bishops of Winchester, Downton and Hindon, never progressed far from their original framework. One, however, which involved moving a community from a cramped and hostile environment to a lush, green-field site was spectacularly successful. This was the removal of the cathedral and its staff from Old Salisbury's hilltop to the confluence of the Avon and Nadder and the creation of a new town and market around it.

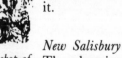

Richard Poore, Bishop of Salisbury 1217-28, who laid the foundation stone of the new cathedral in 1220

New Salisbury

The planning of the new town was given much thought. Precise plans for the layout of the buildings in its Close were approved by the Chapter in 1213, Pope Honorius III was asked to sanction the move in 1217 and

50

his bull approving it was issued in 1219. A churchyard was consecrated, a temporary wooden chapel was erected, a residence for the bishop was completed and construction of the new cathedral begun in 1220.

The foundation stones were laid by Bishop Richard Poore, the greatest driving force in the enterprise, and by the Sheriff, William Longespée and his Countess Ela. By 1225 the east end had been completed and three altars consecrated. There was a slight hiccup in the building about 1244, for the pope had to grant indulgences to those willing to contribute to its completion, but it was consecrated in 1258 in the presence of King Henry III, who had himself been generous in his gifts to the church. In

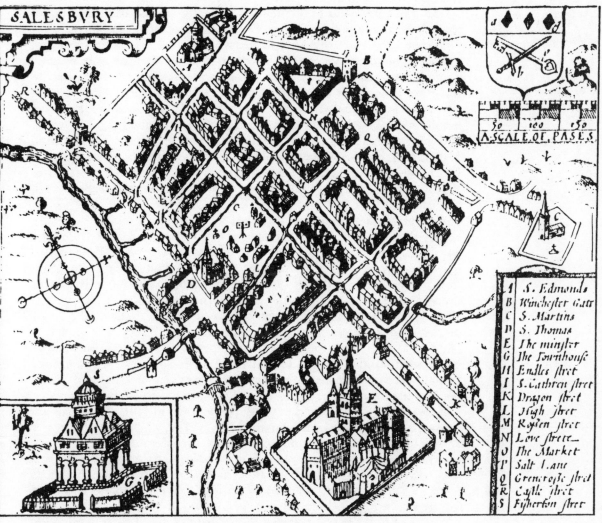

Fig. 5. Salisbury, from John Speed's atlas, 1610.

51

The belfry tower, Salisbury Cathedral. The spire was pulled down in 1768 and the rest about 1789

1266 its lead roofing and its separate belfry tower to the north were complete. It was now the most unified in style of all the English cathedrals, having been completed, except for the spectacular central tower and spire added about 1334, within 60 years.

Salisbury Cathedral was an ideal expression of the 'Early English' style, severely rectangular in plan with clearly separate parts, two pairs of transepts, all chapels facing east, a prominent north porch and a screen at the western end wider than nave and aisles and covered with sculpture. It was intended by its designers Nicholas of Ely and Canon Elias of Dereham, to be seen as it still is, in a sea of green with canonical houses round the fringe of its large Close, where both designers resided.

The size and layout of the new town were generous and much larger than those of any previous town. Eighty-three acres were allotted to the Close and 120 for urban development, with another 57 acres of somewhat marshy ground east of the Close kept in reserve. Hindon only covered about thirty acres overall. The layout was determined by a wish to maintain privacy for the Close and the need to provide water to most streets by little canals from the River Avon. It was modified to fit the hamlet of St Martin, which was then confusingly called the 'old town', and the major existing roads, of which the most important was that from Milton Hill to a ford over the Avon at Fisherton Bridge. The whole site had to be above general flood level and within easy reach of its water supply, which was eventually taken from the leat to the bishop's mill at Fisherton.

A large market-place was provided at the junction of the two older roads, the east-west from Winchester to Wilton and that from Old Salisbury, and the main building blocks, which have been called 'chequers' since the 15th century at least, were laid out in rectangular form to the north and east of the market-place. The Close itself was divorced and protected from the town by the Close Ditch, which was its chief defence until the building of the Close wall in the second quarter of the 14th century. The north-south Endless Street was probably planned as a through route to a river crossing south of the town, so as to by-pass the older line of Castle Street and High Street which continued straight through the Close, but Endless Street was severed by defences north of the town and never developed the importance of the older route.

A new bridge was provided south of the town in 1240, the Harnham Bridge, now called by its later name of Aylswade, which provided easier access to the south-west and contributed considerably to the relative decay of Wilton. A new hospital of St Nicholas to care for the poor, sick and travellers was built about 1230 and a university college, the de Vaux or Valley college, was founded in 1260. This new college attracted teachers of a high calibre as well as students from Oxford and Cambridge, and it has been suggested that Salisbury might have rivalled the older universities if the rent of rooms made high by its commercial success had not put off the poorer students.

As it was, the success of New Salisbury was soon manifest. In the poll tax returns for 1377, 3,226 names were recorded for New Salisbury and only 10 for Old.

An industrial revolution

Increasing export of wool and other agricultural products through Bristol to the west and through Southampton to the south-east added to the prosperity generated in the county by the success of its new market centre, while the young and ill-organised cloth industry was spreading through old and new towns and then out into the countryside to escape the restrictions of urban taxation and guilds. Wool and corn had for long kept Wiltshire prosperous; the growth of the woollen cloth industry was to make it part of the most industrialised area in the country. At the tax assessment of 1225, in the time of Henry III, Wiltshire was fourteenth in wealth of the English counties. By 1334, under Edward III, it had risen to twelfth, while the new city of Salisbury was now the country's twelfth richest town.

The main cause was a revolution in the West Country caused by the introduction and spread of fulling mills. Up to the end of the 12th century the spinning of wool was done by spinsters, women working at home, the weaving by men on a single loom, also at home, while the cleaning and felting was done by 'walkers' (later called fullers or tuckers) who trod the cloth for hours in tubs filled with water, stale urine and fullers' earth. Right at the end of the century there was a spread up the Wiltshire and Somerset rivers of fulling mills which made the latter processes easier and cheaper and led to the profitable vertical integration of the cloth industry. Such mills usually involved only the simple conversion of water-driven corn-mills by the substitution of large trip hammers for the more complicated gearing, wheels and stones of the corn-grinders to produce machines which could undertake the heavy and continuous process of felting.

The first documentary evidence for such mills in Wiltshire is at Stanley Abbey near Chippenham in 1189, but a royal mill at Elcot near Marlborough which was rebuilt in 1237 may be as old. By the late 13th century there were other such mills at Downton, Mere, Stratford-sub-Castle, near Old Salisbury, Harnham, near New Salisbury, and at Steeple Langford, a few miles up the Wylye.

Clothiers, or clothers, i.e. those who organised the manufacture of woollen cloth, were by the end of the 12th century becoming as unpopular as millers and attempts were made to control their trade and their ambitions; by a 'Law of Weavers and Fullers' which applied to Beverley, Oxford, Winchester and Marlborough they were prevented from becoming freemen of those towns, though such inhibitions only promoted an exodus to the country areas. Thus Bedwyn, Marlborough and Cricklade, which had been early cloth-making centres, soon lost ground to rural areas while Salisbury remained a centre for another four centuries but

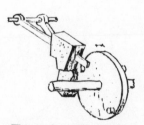

The simple mechanism of fulling stocks, tripped by cams on the drive shaft to pound the cloth in troughs below

53

was sustained more and more by its prosperous markets. Meanwhile fulling mills spread from Salisbury up the River Wylye and up the Bristol Avon and its tributary the By Brook.

Owners of fulling mills started integrating the industry in the 13th and 14th centuries by buying wool from its major producers or from wool-staplers, sending it out as piece-work to women spinners, sending the spun yarn as piece-work to male weavers and bringing it back to their mills for cleaning, felting and stretching. They then sold it as white cloth through local markets, or exported it; the London-based Merchant Adventurers Company came to command a near monopoly through their London headquarters at Blackwell Hall. As demand for coloured and then fancy cloths arose, the fullers sent the cloths to dyers and finishing shops, which they often owned themselves. Such changes, however, took some centuries to complete and their main trade was in white cloth, usually 'broadcloth' two yards in width.

Decline and plague

There were bad times in the 14th century. The expansion of the population and the encroachment of arable farming onto marginal land meant that more and more people lived at subsistence levels and were prone to famine in times of bad harvest. A run of bad harvests occurred in the early 14th century and brought widespread starvation; the same period saw epidemic disease in farm animals. On the Winchester estates in south-east Wiltshire the number of oxen was halved in the 1320s and there was a decline in the amount of arable land on most big estates during the century. At Durrington it fell from 300 acres in 1324 to 213 in 1359, while at Downton it declined from over 800 in 1208 to 300 in 1347. Part of this decline in acreage was due to the simultaneous expansion of wool and cloth export markets which increased the demand for sheep runs at the expense of arable land. But prices were also beginning to fall by the middle of the 14th century and the growth of the population slowed or stopped.

Into a period of agricultural depression and only two years after the spectacular English victory over the French at Crécy (1346), the greatest plague in European history reached this country. This was the bubonic plague known as the 'Black Death', which entered Wessex through Melcombe Regis in the summer of 1348 and then through Bristol and other ports, on flea-infested rats, and spread rapidly through the country. Its effect was dramatic, particularly on the undernourished peasants, though it was no respecter of lords and priests. Of tenants on the Glastonbury Abbey estates in Wiltshire some fifty-five per cent died. Of the canons of Ivychurch Priory, south of Salisbury, 13 out of the 14 died and at Durrington, which may have been a more typical estate, 18 of the 41 tenants died. 'God is deaf nowadays', said a priest, 'prayers have no powere the plague to stay', and it was a terrifying time. The plague

Monument to John Stokys, clothier, died 1498, in Holy Cross, Seend

54

returned in later years and following centuries, but never with such devastating effect.

Apart from a widespread reduction in the population and the occasional disappearance of a medieval hamlet, which was more common in Dorset and Somerset, the chief consequences were the shortage of labour, the rise in real wages resulting from competition for the services of the survivors and the freedom given to landless but land-tied peasants to seek their fortunes elsewhere.

The Ordinances and Statute of Labourers were passed by Parliament in 1349 and 1351 at the request of a new middle-class of smaller gentry and larger tenant-farmers, to make it illegal for farm-labourers to accept wages higher than they were two years before the plague. These laws could be and were ignored by the younger landless peasants, who could leave their manors, to which they were legally bound, and find work and better wages elsewhere from an employer who would not ask too many questions, but it was impossible for a married man with children, who could not leave home and whose cost of provisions would now exceed his wages, to ignore them.

The combination of restrictions and attempted enforcement of them contributed to the Peasants' Revolt of 1381 in which labourers from south-east England captured London, murdered the Archbishop of Canterbury and were only dispersed after false promises from King Richard II. The revolt, however, had little effect on Wiltshire where most of the provisions of the new laws were presumably ignored, as only minor troubles are recorded in manor court rolls, such as that tenants at Urchfont refused to make beer for the Abbess of St Mary, Winchester, and tenants at Malmesbury left town in the autumn to avoid gathering the lord's harvest.

Parks

There was a considerable increase in parkland during the 14th century and much of it may have been associated with rural depopulation. Colerne had a new park of 200 acres by 1311, Castle Combe one by 1328, which was raided for its rabbits by local parsons in 1392. There were other new parks, two at Vastern near Wootton Bassett in 1334, at Oakwood in 1347, Lydiard Tregoze in 1348 and Everleigh in 1361 while two areas were added to an existing park at Rowcombe near Tisbury. In a slightly different category was Aldbourne's great chase which was producing rabbits by the thousand, nearly a thousand, worth £14, being supplied for the royal household in 1434. Increases in timber, hunting or rabbits were, however, small compared with the growth and rationalisation of the wool and woollen-cloth industry.

Towns: the 14th century

Before dealing further with the devlopment of the cloth industry a word should be said about the towns in the 14th century. Unfortunately we

Alys Stokys, wife of John Stokys

55

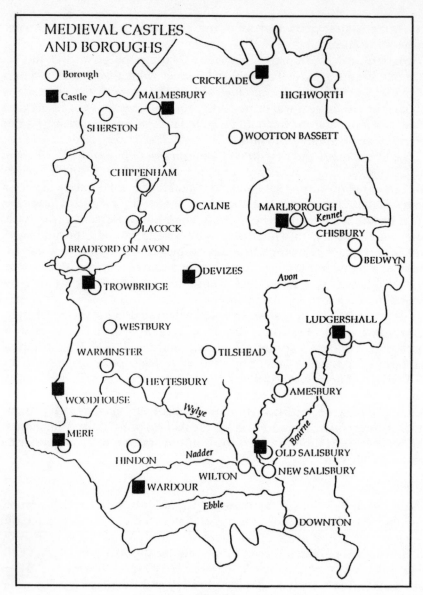

Map 7.

have no comparable figures for Wiltshire towns before and after the Great Plague but we have some which show their relative importance in the 2nd and 4th quarters of the century. The first list is a valuation of movable property in towns and other places, the second the number of poll-tax payers. The two lists may be subject to gross inaccuracies

56

and cannot be used with confidence to indicate the changes in individual towns over the century: we can only be sure of the unchallenged position of Salisbury which in each count has a value five times larger than any other place.

In 1334 the first 15 in order of valuation for taxation were:

'Town'	£s value	'Town'	£s value
Salisbury	7,500	Mere	157
Bremhill	232	Aldbourne	155
Corsham	225	Charlton nr Downton	150
Wanborough	210	Amesbury	146
Donhead & hamlets	198	Hannington	140
West Lavington	180	Tisbury	135
Chippenham Boro'	173	Potterne	130
Melksham	157		

In 1377 the top 15 towns by numbers of poll-tax payers were

'Town'	Number of payers	'Town'	Number of payers
Salisbury	3,226	Corsham	341
Wilton	639	Warminster	340
Melksham	511	Longbridge Deverill	322
Mere	489	Purton	318
Marlborough	462	Devizes	302
Malmesbury	402	Tisbury	281
Donhead	359	Damerham (now Hants)	271
Lacock	355		

Near the end of the 14th century Wiltshire was probably tenth of English counties in population, as it had been at the time of the Domesday survey in 1086, but fourth in taxable capacity. Its apparent wealth was due largely to the successful cloth industry of Salisbury.

Wool

The rationalisation of the supply of wool was led by the Hungerfords, who had estates across the county from Mildenhall in the east to Wellow and Farleigh (Hungerford) in Somerset. They made Heytesbury in the Wylye valley their main breeding centre in the 14th century and later their main rearing centre for lambs brought or sent up to thirty miles to and from other manors. The same specialisation was shown on the Glastonbury Abbey estates and on those of the bishops of Winchester. Heytesbury remained for many years the main wool warehouse of the Hungerford manors and an important wool store even when the Hungerfords moved their estate headquarters to Farleigh in Somerset. The Winchester manors sent their wool to places in Hampshire and the Glastonbury estates sent theirs into Somerset.

Both Hungerford and Winchester estates kept flocks of over a thousand sheep on many of their manors and the Glastonbury flocks were often little smaller. But in the late 14th century there was another big slump in farm prices and from then until late in the next century the large landowners withdrew from direct farming and relied on the renting of

The Poultry Cross, Salisbury

57

land, rather than sale of wool and grain, to maintain their incomes. The position of the smaller tenant, whether serf or freeman, improved during the 15th century as he was able to acquire low-rented additional land and to escape from the burden of forced labour on the lord of the manor's demesne.

Cloth

The pattern of the cloth-making industry was changing. In a table of cloths approved by 'aulnagers', the court officials appointed to enforce standard measure and collect tax on cloth, of the time of Henry V, i.e. in the early 15th century, Salisbury was still much the most dominant producer with 1,309 cloths approved in one year, though some of these may have been brought into Salisbury by producers from up the Wylye valley. Nearby Wilton is credited with only 67 cloths, Devizes with 140, the Warminster area with 129, Mere with 80 and Castle Combe with seventy-one. Production was moving west.

Castle Combe, in the north-west corner of the county, is now the most picturesque village in Wiltshire, but its industrial growth in the 15th century affords the most dramatic illustration of the new industry. It was on a fast-flowing tributary of the Avon, the By Brook, not too distant from the port of Bristol and close to the source of the best English wool, the Cotswolds. Under the lordship of the Norfolk knight, Sir John Fastolf (a name that may have suggested Falstaff to Shakespeare), three fulling mills, a gig-mill for mechanical shearing of cloth, fifty new houses and a church tower decorated with symbols of the cloth industry were all built within the first half of the century. Sir John equipped his own men-at-arms to fight in France in a livery of red and white cloth made at Castle Combe, and for this purpose bought there up to a thousand yards of cloth a year. His village, alone among Wiltshire cloth producers, became famous for its red dyes, and cloth was sent there from Bath and Cirencester for dyeing. 'Castlecombes' were soon recognised as a trade name for these red-dyed woollens. The county was not otherwise renowned for its dyeing, though the fine striped cloth of Salisbury known as Rays was already famous.

Before the end of the 15th century the industry had spread over the whole of West Wiltshire and now stretched from Malmesbury to Westbury, and from Bradford to Devizes, an area that was now looking more to Bristol than to London for its sales.

The Church

Monastic life in the one and half centuries after the Black Death was maintained but with less enthusiasm and less public support. The number of monks declined and only in the nunneries, which were tending to become a refuge for unmarried women of 'gentle' birth, was there pressure on available accommodation. There was some limited revolt

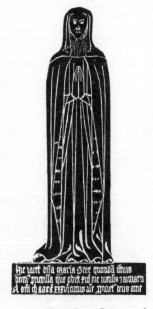

Mary Gore, Prioress of Amesbury, died 1436

against the luxury of Church and monasteries; the early Protestant movement known as Lollardy became popular at the end of the 14th century and was supported by John Montague, Earl of Salisbury, although he was made to make public penance to his bishop. Early in the next century two men were prosecuted by the Church for spreading Protestant doctrines. But economic grievances were often centred on Church property and at the time of the unrest associated with Jack Cade's popular revolt of 1450, a crowd attacked the cathedral at Salisbury and there were other attacks on Church property at Biddestone, Devizes, Tilshead and Wilton. Later on the same day as the attack at Salisbury, a mob led by men from that town dragged Bishop Ayscough from the priory church of Edington. He was unpopular for he was also the king's chaplain and adviser. In the words of the contemporary account:

The arms of Edington Priory

> William Ascoghe . . . was slayn of his owen parisshens and peple . . . after that he had said Masse and was drawn from the auter and led up to an hill ther beside, in his awbe and his stole aboute his necke; and ther they slew him horribly, their fader and their bisshope, and spoilid him unto the nakid skyn, and rente his blody shirte in to pecis.

The mob went on to plunder the priory. Nevertheless Wiltshire was predominantly conservative in church matters though there were seeds of Protestantism in the manufacturing west, which would welcome the reforms of the next century.

Monuments

The Wiltshire clothiers left their mark on the county's churches. The churches of St Thomas and of St Edmund at Salisbury were completely rebuilt by the town's richer merchants. St Mary's at Devizes was rebuilt for another cloth merchant, the church at Seend was given a fine north aisle by the clothier John Stokys, who had the cloth-maker's shears carved on its wall, and Trowbridge church was largely rebuilt for two rich clothiers. The most notable building is perhaps the church of Steeple Ashton, one of the most handsome and richly ornamented in the county, which was largely rebuilt for two clothiers, Robert Long and Walter Lucas, between 1480 and 1500, and designed and built by a mason who was another clothier. Many large and elaborate porches were added to churches at this time, as it had become the custom for much business to be conducted in such places.

In addition, newly-rich clothiers built substantial manor houses. The most unified and attractive is the manor house at Great Chalfield, built by Thomas Tropenell at the end of the 15th century. Others are South Wraxall, probably built for Robert Long, and Westwood Manor, built for Thomas Horton, the clothier of Bradford who also built the best tower in the county on his parish church next door.

Westwood Manor

VI Tudor Wiltshire

Robert Baynard of Lackham, near Lacock, died 1501

In the dynastic quarrel which was later called the 'Wars of the Roses' by the romantic novelist Walter Scott, Wiltshire men took little interest and the county was lucky that the fighting affected it so little. Richard III had caused some raised eyebrows in Salisbury by having the Duke of Buckingham summarily executed on a Sunday but when the wars ended with his own death in 1485 the news was probably received in Wiltshire with the indifference shown by the 'Chronicle of London', which reported it between news of a sheriff's death and of an outbreak of plague.

In 1497, when Henry VII was well established as monarch, there was little local interest in a threatened invasion by the Scots in support of a pretender to the throne, Perkin Warbeck, and when Cornishmen rebelling against taxes imposed to finance a war against Scotland (and led by the Wiltshire landowner James Touchet, 7th Baron Audley) marched across the county to defeat at Blackheath, Wiltshire men neither joined nor molested them. Again when Perkin himself landed later that year in the west, Wiltshire people stayed aloof though they provided forced levies which thwarted his siege of Exeter. Nevertheless they were fined by Henry's General Daubeny for their alleged support of Perkin. They were, of course, more concerned with farm rents and the price of corn, and particularly with the prices of wool and cloth, the chief exports of the county.

Inside Wiltshire the older important families were in relative decline and, while they still held substantial estates, most had lost political power. This was true of the Hastings, who held 14 manors in the county, the Wests, who held 12, the Willoughby de Brokes, who held 11, and the Stourtons, who held 17, and all held extensive lands outside Wiltshire. The eminence of the last ended dramatically in 1557 when the then Lord Stourton, who had been insanely jealous of the rising newcomers, was hung for the murder of his own steward. The Hungerfords, who had a sheep empire stretching from Berkshire to Somerset, held and extended their own until Sir Walter Hungerford, made Baron Hungerford in 1536, was executed in 1540 for supporting Henry VIII's discredited minister Cromwell. In addition the Seymours, who had acquired the Savernake estate following the extinction of the Sturmys and had their principal house at Wolf Hall near Great Bedwyn, also prospered, for Sir Edward Seymour's sister Jane became Henry's third queen and produced his only male heir. When this child became King

Jane Seymour (1509-37), third queen of Henry VIII

Edward VI at the age of 11, Seymour, already made Earl of Hertford by Henry, became Duke of Somerset and then Lord Protector, but he was judicially murdered by political rivals in 1552, though not before he amassed vast estates at the expense of the Church.

One other family, that of the Herberts, was new to the county and has been of importance to it ever since. William Herbert, a favourite of Henry VIII's, was knighted in 1543 and made Earl of Pembroke and Lord Lieutenant in 1551, obtained the Abbey of Wilton and its extensive estates in 1542 and 1544, and was even more enriched when monastic lands formerly in the hands of the Seymours were granted him. The jealous Lord Stourton would sound his horn derisively whenever he passed the gates of Herbert's Wilton House, said Aubrey. Lord Stourton was also particularly jealous of another newcomer, John Thynne, a protégé of the Seymours, who built a large house hidden in the park of the former Longleat Priory.

Edward Seymour of Wolf Hall, near Bedwyn, 1st Duke of Somerset, executed 1552

The economy

The population of the country rose throughout the 16th century, though there was some interruption in its rise during the unsettling reign of Henry VIII's elder daughter Mary, and her joint rule with Philip of Spain, due to an epidemic of 'sweating sickness', perhaps influenza. But to Wiltshire more worrying was the continuous and sharply rising inflation which was made worse by the debasement of the coinage under both Henry and his son Edward. Prices rose faster than wages throughout the period and farm prices rose some five times, twice as fast as farm wages. The price of wool, on which so much of Wiltshire's farm and industrial trade depended, rose about three times. As so often this made the smart and rich richer and the poor poorer.

Cloth

The county's cloth industry had lost some ground during the preceding (15th)century, not only to that of East Anglia but also to those of Somerset and Devon, which were somewhat more sensitive to demands for less traditional and lighter cloths. Partly as a consequence, Wiltshire had slipped to sixth county in England in taxable capacity, as is shown by the 'lay subsidies' (taxes based on income and land together) of 1523-7, whereas it had been fourth in 1377. From now on Wiltshire declined in the league-table of English counties judged by population or wealth.

The former export of wool had shrunk as a result of royal taxation on its export and by the increased demand from the growing cloth industry. Wiltshire's own wool was rarely of top quality; the best came from the Welsh Borders or the Cotswolds. But in spite of trouble with wool and competition from other cloth areas Wiltshire remained a principal producer and exporter of cloth.

Most of the output was now sold through merchants based at

Double-wheeled plough used on flinty soils, 1515

61

*Merchant's mark of
Jerome Poticary of
Stockton, died 1596,
brother-in-law of John
Topp, builder of
Stockton House*

Blackwell (once Bakewell) Hall, headquarters of the rising Company of Merchant Adventurers which had superseded the Merchant Staplers, who had previously monopolised wool exports, as the chief export earners of the country. Most cloth from Wiltshire was made up into large bundles and sent to London on packhorses by way of the 'Bath' road via Devizes and Marlborough. Distribution and outlets can be judged from surviving account books of the merchants and are particularly illuminated by those of John Kitson of the London Merchant Adventurers and of John Smythe, an independent merchant from Bristol, in the early 16th century. They show that cloth manufacture was then concentrated in west Wiltshire from Malmesbury to Longbridge Deverill, and spread over the Somerset border and down the Frome valley. The Wiltshire clothiers were largely dependent on the Adventurers' market for both direct sale and overseas export, to which half their product went, but some cloth made on the Somerset border went to Bristol where a few merchants controlled dyeing and finishing works and exported to growing markets in western France and Spain.

Cloth was still made at Salisbury and Wilton but its sale was divided between London and the local market, which also imported dyes and oils for the finishing processes, while some was exported through Southampton to northern France. Production in this area appears to have declined, but thanks to its succesful markets Salisbury was the sixth wealthiest town in England in the early 16th century, behind only London, Norwich, Bristol, Newcastle and Coventry. Its population reached about eight thousand in the 1520s but with the decline in its cloth industry, this fell to about seven thousand by the end of the century. It was then only fifteenth among the leading towns. Away from these main areas there was a resurgence of the cloth industry up the Kennet valley as far as Marlborough, at the time when Jack Winchcombe, 'Jack of Newbury', was successfully producing cloth at Newbury (Berks.).

Many Wiltshire clothiers were now not only prosperous but respected, like the Hortons of Westwood of whom the elder Thomas endowed both a chantry and school at Bradford on Avon and made his successor and heir, his nephew Thomas the younger, one of the richest men in the county by 1545. The latter's daughters married into other clothing families which included the Longs of Whaddon and the Winchcombes of Newbury. By the end of the century the Hortons had become 'gentry' and left the cloth trade, as also had the Longs, Methuens and Yerburys. The most enterprising of the new rich clothiers, however, was William Stumpe of Malmesbury, who claimed some intimacy with the king and was the richest man in Malmesbury and one of the Abbey tenants before its dissolution.

The rape of the monasteries

After the number of Henry VIII's wives, the 'dissolution' of the monasteries is the most memorable event in the Tudor 'Reformation'. The two

62

were of course connected, for it was difficulties with the Pope, as head of the Church, over Henry's proposed divorce from Queen Katherine, who had not produced a male heir, that drove Henry to take over control of the Church and of Church property in England.

Confiscation of monastic property was not new. 'Foreign' houses, which owed allegiance to headquarters overseas as did Ogbourne Priory (and its manor of Brixton Deverill) in 1435 to the Norman Abbey of Bec, were confiscated as enemy property when kings went to war, while Cardinal Wolsey had already arbitrarily confiscated the Abbey of Osney, near Oxford, to help build his Cardinal College (now Christ Church) in that city.

Cardinal Thomas Wolsey (c.1475-1530), Lord Chancellor to Henry VIII

The Reformation of the Church followed slowly after the suppression of monasteries. There had been 'Protestant' movements to simplify ceremonies, reduce the importance of images and introduce the Bible to the common man, but they did not get far in Wiltshire and as late as 1518 two 'Lollards' (followers of John Wycliffe) were executed at Salisbury.

Six years after this the Pope, at Henry's request, appointed Cardinal Campeggio, the papal legate, as Salisbury's only foreign bishop. In 1529 Campeggio and Wolsey were appointed to consider the question of the king's divorce. Campeggio managed to defer the inquiry long enough to escape to Rome but Wolsey was disgraced after his failure to obtain the annulment. His successor Thomas Cromwell set himself to subject the Church to the king and at the same time to replenish the treasury which had been exhausted by court extravagance at home and abroad. Much of his plan depended on the suppression of the religious houses through-out the country and in this he succeeded. In Wiltshire, apart from the decayed priory at Longleat which had been appropriated by the Hinton Charterhouse (Somerset) a few years earlier, all were functioning in 1535. By December 1539 none were left.

It was all done legally, step by step, with the help of a pliant or terrorised Parliament. The Acts for the Restraint of Appeals to the Pope and for the Submission of the Clergy were passed, which declared the supremacy of the king over the Church not as a new principle but as one which had previously been obscured by the Pope's pretension. The rights of visitation and appointments were transferred from the Pope to the king. Cromwell was then appointed Vicar-General and thus empowered to visit and value all religious property in the country. The resulting survey, the '*Valor Ecclesiasticus*', showed that it totalled over £300,000 a year or ten per cent of the kingdom's revenue and that half of this belonged to monastic and religious orders. Relatively to the whole kingdom the value of religious property had in fact fallen by about half since the late 13th century. But whatever the value in real terms, it illustrated what is known from other sources, that religious houses had been disposing of their property for ready money and to

Thomas Cromwell (c.1485-1540), Vicar-General, 1535

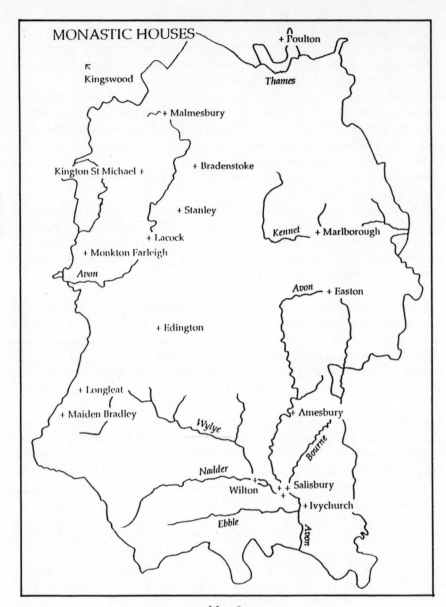

MONASTIC HOUSES

Poulton

Kingswood

Thames

+ Malmesbury

+ Bradenstoke

Kington St Michael +

+ Stanley

+ Lacock

+ Monkton Farleigh

Avon

Kennet + Marlborough

Avon + Easton

+ Edington

+ Longleat

+ Maiden Bradley

Wylye

+ Amesbury

Bourne

Nadder

+ + Salisbury
Wilton +
+Ivychurch

Ebble

Avon

Map 8.

provide for their own rising standard of living when popular support and the number of monks and nuns had been declining. Only at Lacock of the Wiltshire houses was there an exception, for here its value had doubled, to about three times the average of such houses.

19. The beautiful manor house at Great Chalfield, built by Thomas Tropenell at the end of the 15th century – now National Trust property.

20. Lake House, in the Avon Valley north of Salisbury. This flint and stone house was built about 1580 for George Duke, a clothier.

21. Malmesbury Abbey. The nave of this once massive church was given to the town by the clothier Thomas Stumpe after the dissolution of the important monastery. St Aldhelm had been its second abbot.

22. Lacock Abbey, in 1808; a watercolour by John Buckler. The abbey was bought at the Dissolution by William Sharington, master of the king's mint at Bristol. The first photograph in the world, of an oriel window at Lacock, was taken by his descendant, William Henry Fox Talbot, in 1839.

23. The south front of Corsham Court, built by Thomas Smythe of London in 1582 and bought by Paul Methuen of Bradford on Avon in 1745.

24. Longleat, the south front, built by Sir John Thynne between 1568 and 1580.

25. Holy Trinity, Easton Royal, the only Tudor church in Wiltshire. It was built in 1591 by Sir Edward Seymour, Earl of Hertford, following the demolition of the former friary church there. Seymour monuments in the latter were transferred to the church at Great Bedwyn.

26. Wardour Old Castle, which changed hands twice during the Civil War. It was refurbished by Robert Smythson in the late 16th century, and its owners, the Arundell family, built a magnificent Georgian house nearby in 1770-6, leaving the old castle as a romantic ruin.

27. Gateway, Fonthill Gifford, built in the early 17th century for 'Fonthill Splendens', the predecessor of Fonthill Abbey. Its design has been attributed to Inigo Jones.

The number of inmates and the estimated annual income of the chief houses in Wiltshire revealed by the *Valor* was as follows:

House	Inmates	Annual income £
Malmesbury (*Benedictine*)	24	804
Amesbury (*Benedictine nunnery*)	34	554
Wilton (*Benedictine nunnery*)	32	653
Kington St Michael (*Benedictine nunnery*)	3	38
Monkton Farleigh (*Cluniac*)	6	223
Kingswood [now in Glos.] (*Cistercian*)	15	254
Stanley (*Cistercian*)	10	223
Bradenstoke (*Austin Canons*)	14	271
Maiden Bradley (*Austin Canons*)	8	198
Ivychurch (*Austin Canons*)	5	133
Lacock (*Austin Canonesses*)	17	204
Edington (*Bonhommes*)	13	522
Easton (*Trinitarian Canons*)	2	56
Poulton (*Gilbertines*)	3	20
Marlborough St Margaret (*Gilbertines*)	5	39

The value of the Wiltshire houses was about three per cent of the total for the kingdom.

Cromwell's chief visitors were Doctors Layton and Legh, one coarse and relishing scandal, the other cold, proud and unpopular with his colleagues. The tendentious reports of their perfunctory visits were given to the king and on the basis of these, often refuted by more careful commissions later, an act was passed in 1536 for the suppression of the smaller monasteries. The Court of Augmentations (of the royal income) was set up to receive the property of all those with an annual income below £200. Commissions of six were then set up for each county and the Wiltshire commission reported on those at Maiden Bradley, Monkton Farleigh, Lacock, Kingston, Stanley, Easton, Ivychurch, Poulton and Marlborough. They had little reason to be partial to the monasteries yet gave them an almost uniformly good character, even in cases where Layton and Legh had been most damaging. Where, for instance, Layton said that the Prior of Maiden Bradley had six natural children and a licence from the Pope to keep a mistress, the new commission stated that he and his brethren were 'by report of honest conversation'. Lacock was given a licence to continue, though on payment to the court of £200, while the houses at Poulton and Marlborough were allowed to continue because they were cells of a larger Gilbertine priory at Sempringham, but all the others were suppressed.

Following a two years' lull, a further Act of Parliament granted to Henry all the property of religious houses which should 'voluntarily surrender' themselves into his hands. 'Persuasion' followed so successfully that within a year no religious houses were left in Wiltshire, nor

Henry VIII, reigned 1509-47

65

anywhere in the kingdom. The houses at Kingswood, Poulton, Marlborough, Lacock, Wilton and Edington were surrendered in quick succession, but at the two remaining, Malmesbury and Amesbury, a change of head had to be engineered before 'voluntary surrender' was achieved. Pensions were granted to most inmates but the Prioress of Amesbury who had refused to surrender was given nothing, whereas Jane Darrell, who had been Prioress for only two months, was given the handsome pension of £100.

The Commissioners had especially noted the 'great relief' given to surrounding areas by the abbeys of Lacock and Stanley and, despite some envy at the wealth of the houses, their total loss must have been felt greatly. Many were the sole sources of education for their areas. There is, however, no evidence in Wiltshire of the unrest that led to rebellion and peasant revolt in the north and east of England.

The Wiltshire properties were all granted away, usually to eager buyers, in the last 10 years of Henry's life. The courtiers Sir William Seymour and Sir William Herbert did well. Seymour was granted the rich Edington property and the smaller properties of Monkton Farleigh, Easton and Maiden Bradley. Herbert obtained the richer prize of Wilton. Disposals were made at what may then have been considered the going market price, but William Sharington, the master of the king's mint at Bristol and responsible for considerable debasement of the coinage, purchased the buildings of Lacock Abbey at what seems only a few 'years' purchase' and well below its real value. Disposal and re-disposal of monastic lands and buildings created a speculative market in land and many of the gentry bought them second- and third-hand in quick succession. John Thynne, helped by his mentor Seymour, bought nothing direct from the crown but over £200 worth from intermediaries in eight different transactions.

The new land market helped towards a partial revolution by distributing wealth over a wider range of society, right down to John Adlam, a clothier of Westbury, who made the smallest purchase from the crown, a close at Rode (now Somerset but then in Wiltshire) worth 17s. 11d. a year. And it brought new and rising gentry into the county.

Of the men taking over monastic property, the most interesting was the above-mentioned William Stumpe, the second-generation clothier of Malmesbury who already leased some of the abbey lands. He paid the comparatively large sum of £1,517 for the abbey and some of its land, granted to the town the nave of the abbey church for use as a parish church, and then filled the rest of the site with looms for weaving cloth, from which he was turning out some three thousand cloths a year by the time of Leland's visit in 1542. Stumpe was a Member for Malmesbury at the 'Reformation' Parliament, was High Collector for North Wiltshire of the king's benevolence in 1545, when he was described as 'gentleman' by reason of his property qualification, and was by far the richest man in the town, even though not in the county's top fifty. He was not content with his Malmesbury factory where he had hoped to build a street of houses across the abbey cloisters, for he intended to rent Osney Abbey (Oxford) and to employ two thousand workers there – a scheme which did not proceed. He invested wealth in land so successfully, however, that his son could be knighted in his own lifetime and his three granddaughters marry three earls.

Butter churning, from the Grete Herball *(1527)*

The treatment of the other houses varied. Lacock was converted to a grand house by Sharington, though he pulled down all of the church but the north wall. Remains of the priory at Longleat were also converted to a house by John Thynne, though it was destroyed in a fire not long after and the present great house was built on the site. A new house was built by the Herberts at Wilton, where only a few fragments of monastic buildings remain. The smaller building at Edington was converted into a more modest house but the others were converted to baser uses and most decayed, particularly because the king's commissioners took the lead from their roofs.

The Reformation

There was little 'reform' in the early stages of Henry's revolutionary moves but there was immediate effect on other churches and most of all on the cathedral church of Salisbury. The bishop and dean were now appointed by the crown and the chapter came more and more under the thumb of Cromwell. Complaints by its members about the king's divorce led to their removal and when one of the canons, Dr. Powell, refused to acknowledge the king's supremacy over the Church he was hung, drawn and quartered. The chapter suffered also from the loss of those prebends which had been attached to monasteries, but most serious of all was deliberate damage to the cathedral itself. In 1539 two men were employed for 50 days to destroy the shrine of St Osmund, the Bishop of Salisbury from 1078 to 1099 whom the chapter had laboured until 1457 to get canonised, and to send all its jewels to the king's treasury.

In 1547 and 1548, following an act of Edward VI's first parliament for the abolition of chantries, the latter were smashed, their priests sacked and their property confiscated, like that of the monasteries, by the Crown. In rural areas such as Heytesbury chantry priests often acted as village schoolmasters and their dispossession was another loss to education in Wiltshire.

Arms of the Diocese of Salisbury

In 1549 a further order was received from the crown for the dispatch of 2,000 marks-worth of the cathedral's plate to the royal mint at Bristol, while during the 1560s and the 1570s the cathedral's stained glass was smashed, probably without any authority, and windows let in wind and rain. An inventory made in 1583 showed that of the cathedral's formerly extensive treasures only 29 items of little value were left.

The changes were not popular and Bishop Shaxton, the reforming

67

bishop appointed by Cromwell to replace Campeggio in 1535, complained two years later to Cromwell that he was still called a heretic by the townspeople who 'hoped to see him burned'. But by the end of his tenure in 1539 the king's orders for the removal of statues and for changes in the services had been accepted in the city, although to its west and over most of the county they were largely ignored. His successor, Bishop Capon, was more pliant and survived the accession, after Edward's early death, of his Catholic sister Mary I; indeed he died in office. A number of Church properties were 'exchanged' by him for the benefit of rapacious courtiers like the Seymours. The Vicar of Bray, immortalised in popular song, was another member of the Salisbury chapter (Berkshire was in the diocese of Salisbury) during the reigns of Henry VIII and Edward VI, but died in 1551 so he cannot have served under Mary. Nevertheless the song, which has more relevance to Bishop Capon, gives some indication of the popular scepticism of its pliant clerics.

The effect of the Reformation and the Counter Reformation under Mary on the rest of the Church was curiously muted and one of ignorance and confusion rather than distress. It took years for churches even in Salisbury to readjust to Protestant directives concerning ritual and was even more difficult for them to adjust under Mary to former rituals which had been so ridiculed by her predecessors. But under Mary a farmer from Bulkington who in 1556 had been teaching a form of Protestantism based on Tyndale's translation of the Bible was burnt with two of his companions, and two years later two farmers from Marlborough narrowly escaped the same fate. In her reign, too, 37 priests who had married were ejected from their parishes. But the greatest resistance to the Counter Reformation came when Mary demanded the return of Church property which had been appropriated not only by the courtiers but by numerous less influential men such as Sharington at Lacock, the St Johns at Lydiard and the Goddards at Castle Eaton, and widely dispersed among even smaller men.

With the accession in 1558 of Henry's Protestant daughter, Elizabeth, matters changed again. Jewel, who had been in exile, succeeded Capon as bishop of Salisbury, and by tireless example and widespread preaching re-introduced discipline into the scattered churches of the diocese. In this he was hampered by the loss of all the monastic and chantry properties and also by the venality of his predecessor. 'Capon has eaten all' he. is reported to have said. He put the diocese in good order, however, and comparative harmony was then maintained down to the time of Laud and Charles I, well into the next century.

To the man in the field the major change in all this 'reformation' was the loss of 43 Holy Days, i.e. holidays, though there was some compensation in the increased importance given to the Sabbath when work (not always defined) was prohibited by law. The Protestant faith

Arms of the Borough of Marlborough, recognised 1565

68

was strengthened with patriotism during the long years when England was threatened with invasion (and renewed religious persecution) from Spain. This danger was acute from about 1580 until well after the dispersal of the 'invincible Armada' in 1588. Preparations for Wiltshire's resistance were in the hands of the Earl of Pembroke, who following the disgrace of the Seymour Duke of Somerset was undisputed master of the county. The county itself was subdivided into military commands under the chief gentry: Sir James Mervyn for the south, Sir John Danvers and Sir Thomas Wroughton for the centre and Sir Henry Knyvett for the north. But apart from lighting of beacons on such high points as Cley Hill to announce the arrival of the Armada, and Pembroke's attendance on the queen with his troop, little other than contribution of funds was demanded of the county. In the special contribution five Wiltshire landowners, Sir Walter Hungerford of Farleigh Castle (Somerset), Edward Horton of Iford, John Hunt of Enford, William Darrell of Littlecote and Sir John Danvers of Dauntsey, paid £50 each. Seventy others, who included Edward Long of Monkton Farleigh, Laurence Hyde of West Hatch, John Thynne of Longleat, Sir Edward Baynton of Bromham and Edmund Ludlow of Hill Deverill, paid £25 each.

Sir John Thynne (1515-80), builder of Longleat House

Monuments

There is little building of the early Tudor period to be seen outside the vernacular architecture of scattered farmhouses, but the reign of Elizabeth was one of great building activity. The first of what Sir John Summerson called the 'Elizabethan prodigy houses' was built at Longleat for Sir John Thynne. As said earlier Thynne got the site of the ruined priory in 1541 and, with the help of well-known craftsmen such as the French carver Alan Maynard, converted the remains into a comfortable house. This he went on improving for over twenty years with the help of the dowry of his wife, sister of the Elizabethan financial wizard Sir Thomas Gresham, whom he had married in 1548. The house was destroyed by fire in 1567 but Thynne started again in 1568 and spent the rest of his life (till 1580) in building the present palace. Much of the new house has been attributed to Robert Smythson, the architect of Wollaton (Notts.) and of the refurbishment of the old Wardour Castle, and he was certainly employed here, but the greater credit for the 'nobel and delicate' design should go to Thynne, who had experience in building Seymour's Somerset House, London, and knew what he wanted at Longleat. It was the first English mansion to have the regular consistent treatment of all facades which marks the true Renaissance. The siting of the great hall is still medieval, but the only external quirk is the eccentric spacing of little domed banquetting rooms on the house's flat roof. It was certainly a revolutionary addition to the conservative Wiltshire scene and Thynne was anxious that it should not be seen by his queen until it was finished.

Little of the first great Wilton House on the abbey site is now visible beyond the great porch attributed to Holbein, as it was so much rebuilt and extended in the 17th and 19th centuries. Mention has already been made of the conversion of Lacock Abbey and the improvement of Wardour Castle undertaken by the Arundells in 1598. Corsham Court was built for a London tax collector in 1582 and Littlecote was largely rebuilt for the Somerset lawyer, Popham, later Chief Justice, who had acquired it from Darrells. One large and eccentric building was done for an older Wiltshire family, the triangular Longford Castle near Salisbury which was completed for the Gorges in 1591. More modest buildings included: Lake House, of about 1580, built for the clothier George Duke, Stockton House for another clothier, John Topp, and Upper Upham, belonging to the Goddards, which was completed in 1599.

There was little church building during the 16th century. In 1591 the Seymours pulled down the former friary church at Easton Royal and built a plain, new, Perpendicular-style parish church, the only new Tudor church in the county.

Salisbury in 1588

70

VII Stuart Wiltshire: Discord and Rebellion

Queen Elizabeth, the last Tudor monarch, died in 1603 leaving England proud but weak, and bequeathing to the Stuart dynasty debts and an inadequate financial system. The benefits of the 'Elizabethan Poor Law' with its 'right to work' and welfare for the disabled were lost beneath the tide of rising population while dissension over religious conformity, made worse by the arbitrary changes of earlier Tudors, undermined the respect for authority which had made Wiltshire in particular cheap and easy to govern.

The 'Old Poor Law', that is the law applying before the 'New Poor Law' of 1834, is commonly considered to be Elizabethan, but in fact its principles go back to an act passed in 1536, when the country was suffering from the activities of bands of ex-servicemen and others trying to find a living. It provided for relief to the 'impotent' poor (previously an obligation of the church) to be given by each parish and for 'sturdy beggars' to be impelled to work or suffer branding and flogging. The parishes were expected to provide relief voluntarily and it was not until 1563 that J.P.s were empowered to raise compulsory funds for poor relief, while the administration was not made formal and uniform until the acts of 1598 and 1601, since christened the 'Elizabethan Poor Law'. It was, admittedly, harsh but was still in advance of provision in most continental countries.

The law was brought into considerable disrepute later by some administrators of the Act of Settlement, passed following the Stuart Restoration, of 1662 which permitted parish overseers of the poor to send back to their native parish (usually the place of birth) any vagrants or others whom the overseers thought might be a charge on the overseers' parish. But even this was not entirely new for in 1582 a child was ordered to be separated from its mother and 'carried from tithing to tithing until it come to the place where it was born, videlicet at Melksham'. Luckily not all paupers were treated with such callousness, but 'settlement' cases of this sort increased as local populations and local unemployment grew.

The 'native' unemployed had to be found work by private indenture, or in a house of correction. Wiltshire had to levy a rate of 4d. in the pound in 1578 to provide such a house. The county tried to obtain part of the royal castle at Devizes for this purpose, but failing that they had to buy other premises in that town and hoped to recoup some of the loss by using the premises also for storing county records.

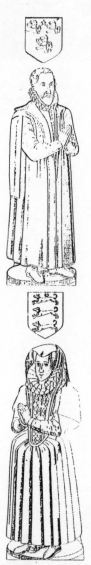

Thomas Bennet (died 1605), and Margaret, his wife, from a brass in Westbury church

71

Thomas Hobbes (1588-1679), political philosopher, born at Malmesbury

In the 17th century Wiltshire was certainly a county of change and Dissent. These were more marked in the Cheese Country of the north and west, where manufacture had been concentrated and population growth had been highest. They were muted in the more traditional and socially better-knit communities of the Chalk Country.

In the second half of the 16th century England's population had grown by about 45 per cent; Wiltshire maintained its share. At the beginning of the 17th century the county's population density (88 persons per square mile) was slightly above the national average, above all its neighbours but Somerset and well above that of Hampshire. The pressure on land was now severe in the Cheese Country and subdivision of land there increased rapidly. Holdings were already small, for in 1590 over half were less than 20 acres in extent; by 1640 three-quarters were below this level.

The increased demand for food, particularly from the manufacturing areas, led to higher grain prices and to the growth of capitalist farming, a change from simple production for subsistence, which was characteristic of much farming under the common-field system, to production for the 'market'. Considerable extra production was achieved by the introduction of water meadows, which needed substantial capital investment in their construction and maintenance. These were meadows artificially watered and flooded in winter from a carefully controlled network of channels. Such flooding protected the grass from frost, while the silt deposited improved its fertility so that, it is estimated, water meadows produced four times as much hay as ordinary meadows. While cattle could sometimes be pastured in the meadows, if they would not damage the drains, the improved economy of the system depended on the greatly increased number of sheep which they could support. Sheep were folded on the meadows in early spring and the hay could feed them over the winter, but for most of the year they were sent out to forage on the sparse grasses of the open downland during the day, and folded at night on the arable, which would thus be fertilised by their dung. A special breed, the now-rare Wiltshire Horned, with a short fleece and long legs, was developed for the purpose and might walk forty miles a day; it was particularly valued as a 'walking dung-cart'. Water meadows were introduced on the Pembroke estates in the Wylye valley in 1632, and spread rapidly.

The growth of market-oriented farming also brought engrossment and inclosure in the corn-growing areas. These changes did little harm to the latter but, together with a fall in dairy prices and government interference in the cloth industry, hit the Cheese Country hard and increased the social divisions in the county. In practical terms it was easier to enlarge and improve the Chalk Country farms and much was done. Even when the Ludlows at Hill Deverill or the Pembrokes of Wilton arbitrarily enclosed large areas of former common fields and

Wiltshire Horned ram

72

turned former plough-owning smallholders into labourers, there was little lasting protest. But in the Cheese Country there was little scope for rationalisation and the few areas of marginal land which might be brought into cultivation were largely in the remnants of the royal forests, which were some of the last disposable assets of the Stuart kings.

The arbitrary enclosure of Melksham Forest from 1607 to 1612, of Pewsham Forest in 1623 and of Selwood and Braydon Forests in 1630 led to increasing disturbances, more and more reinforced by aggrieved holders of common rights from other counties led by the mythical Lady Skimmington. The most severe, at Selwood and Braydon, led to riotous levelling which was actually encouraged by local gentry such as Sir Walter Long of Dauntsey. These gentry were themselves protesting that the Stuart kings were inclosing forests and destroying rights of common in order to sell them to royal favourites who were 'foreigners' or 'Papists', or both. In almost every case the local magistrates were unwilling and almost powerless to prosecute the ringleaders in these popular protests.

Cloth shears

Industrial interference

Government interference in the cloth industry led to further alienation in the manufacturing areas of west Wiltshire and Salisbury. Particular damage was done by the 'Cockayne Project' of 1614. By this James I misguidedly granted to a London Alderman, Cockayne, the right to dye and finish cloth before its export and simultaneously banned the export of undyed cloth. As foreign customers thought poorly of contemporary English finishing and preferred to do their own dyeing, they sought other sources of undyed cloth. The West-Country industry suffered increasingly until in 1617 the scheme was abandoned.

Further resentment was caused in the 1630s by the appointment of government inspectors of cloth, although in this case the action was due to the complaints of London cloth merchants concerning the variable quality of the product. An officious administrator, Anthony Wither, who was sent to enforce the new regulations, was thrown into the river at Bradford in 1632 and the government again had a hard time persuading local magistrates to take any action against the offenders.

The divide between Cheese and Chalk Country was widened further by efforts to enforce religious conformity. Here again Tudor efforts at unification of the kingdom through uniformity in religion led to increased schism under the Stuarts. Two acts passed under Edward VI requiring the use of a new Prayer Book (originally devised by Archbishop Cranmer) were repealed by Mary but a third act under Elizabeth compelled the use of a new Prayer Book only slightly less Protestant than the second of its two Edwardian predecessors and imposed fines of 12d. a week on absentees from church service. Enforcement varied in strictness, but the Elizabethan book was generally accepted and caused little trouble till William Laud, who was already unpopular as a friend of the Duke of Buckingham and considered one of the king's 'evil advisers'

Shearman at work. On the wall hang teasels mounted in 'handles' for raising the nap

George Herbert (1593-1633), poet and parson

by the great parliamentary leader John Pym, was appointed Archbishop of Canterbury in 1635.

Laud made great efforts to raise the standard of learning of the English clergy. In this his work echoed the sentiments of the poet George Herbert, relative of the Pembrokes, who was rector of Fugglestone and Bemerton (adjoining Wilton) from 1630 to 1633, where he wrote his *Priest to the Temple, or the Countrey Parson, his Character and Rule of Life*. Herbert advised the parson to 'be all to his Parish, and not only a Pastour but a Lawyer also and Phisician' and the parishioners to say their Amens thoughtfully and not in a 'slubbering fashion, gaping or scratching the head or spitting'. But Laud was no prig, understood the importance of traditional amusements and favoured the licensing on Sundays of some sports, which James I had done in 1618 and which Charles I reaffirmed in 1633. The proclamation was welcomed in the traditionalist communities of the Chalk Country but resented by the more Puritan and increasingly nonconformist communities of the north-west.

Real trouble began however with attempts to enforce religious conformity and with Laud's insistence on separating parson from congregation and the railing-off of altars, both of which smacked of 'Popery' to some. Wiltshire however did not suffer the troubles that beset Somerset largely because Bishop John Davenant of Salisbury was less officious and less 'Laudian' than his counterpart at Wells. Davenant recognised that discipline in the Church had been weakened by the Reformation and that ecclesiastical courts had lost most of their 'teeth'.

Things were different, however, when the king tried, on Laud's advice, to enforce conformity along English lines on Scotland. It was the king's efforts to raise taxes to fight the Scots in the 'Bishops' Wars' of 1639 and 1640 which led to the general alienation of the county and when calls were made for local levies to fight the Scots they met with a very sullen response. Untrained and near-mutinous troops, assembled at Warminster and at Marlborough, were sent on hastily by the local magistrates to the king at York; from there they soon returned after being routed by better-disciplined and highly-motivated Scots.

The Civil War or 'Great Rebellion'

By 1630 the leaders of Wiltshire were almost wholly opposed to King Charles. He was openly supported only by the Thynnes of Longleat, who were distracted by domestic affairs, by the Arundells of Wardour, who were debilitated by age, by Robert Hyde of Dinton, who at the outbreak of war between king and parliament in 1642 attempted to secure Salisbury, and half-heartedly by the brothers William Seymour (Lord Hertford) of Wolf Hall and Francis Seymour, recently created Baron Seymour of Trowbridge to wean him from the parliamentary cause.

Nevertheless when hostilities broke out in July of 1642 the parliamentary party in the county seemed incompetent if not divided. They were

74

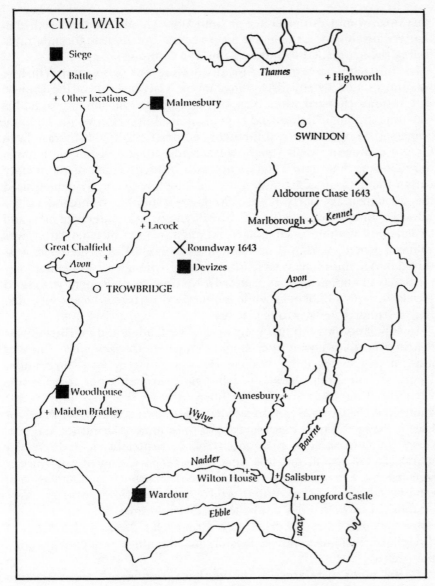

CIVIL WAR

■ Siege

✗ Battle

+ Other locations

Thames

+ Highworth

■ Malmesbury

O SWINDON

✗ Aldbourne Chase 1643

Marlborough + Kennel

+ Lacock

Great Chalfield +

Avon

✗ Roundway 1643

■ Devizes

Avon

O TROWBRIDGE

■ Woodhouse

+ Maiden Bradley

Wylye

Amesbury +

Bourne

Nadder

+ Wilton House

+ Salisbury

■ Wardour

+ Longford Castle

Ebble

Avon

Map 9.

nominally led by the Earl of Pembroke, who had long been associated with the court and as a great collector of art was anxious about his much-beautified house at Wilton. He was indeed so anxious for the latter that Robert Hyde's son Edward, later Earl of Clarendon, said that

75

Malmesbury and Devizes from John Ogilby's road atlas, Britannia *(1675)*

Pembroke would rather either or both sides should be destroyed than that Wilton should be taken. He was of course not alone in this neutralist feeling, which tended to grow as the war continued.

At this stage, however, anti-royalist feeling was strong and Wiltshire was untroubled by royalists, who moved westward out of the county. But fortunes changed when the king concentrated his forces around his war-time capital of Oxford and appointed Sir Ralph Hopton (of Witham, Somerset) as commander of the Army of the West. Royalist forays from Oxford captured Marlborough in December 1642 and Malmesbury in the following February. These successes brought much of the county within the area of 'contribution' to the king and generally demoralised the parliamentary party there. The latter's military commanders, Sir Edward Hungerford and Sir Edward Baynton, proved incompetent and treacherous both to each other and their cause. But the latter was stiffened when in March parliament's General Waller marched west through Wiltshire and retook Malmesbury (though it was almost immediately abandoned by Hungerford). In May Prince Rupert, with Lord Hertford, raided Salisbury while Hungerford besieged the aged royalist Lady Arundell in Wardour Castle.

In July Hopton, with his Army of the West, advanced on Bristol, was defeated at Lansdowne and sought refuge in Devizes where he was immediately besieged by Waller. He was relieved by a force under Henry Wilmot from Oxford, which won a surprising but considerable victory at Roundway outside the town. All the West fell into royalist hands and Devizes was not threatened again until late in 1645. Wardour Castle changed hands twice and there were minor skirmishes and successes for both sides in 1643 and 1644. In September of 1644 Waller marched west again, but this time to defeat in Cornwall and retreat, pursued by a royal army which entered Salisbury in October and established garrisons at Wilton and Longford. More garrisons were established by both sides but neither side could hold Wiltshire for long, not even after Fairfax's drive with Cromwell's New Model Army of disciplined Puritans to relieve Bristol took him almost unopposed across the county.

At this point there arose in the southern counties a loose association of independent neutralists, mostly from Wiltshire and Dorset, who called themselves 'Men of the Club' and met, resolved to try to prevent the ravages of 'foreign armies' of either complexion. Their chief grievances concerned particularly the undisciplined brutality of Goring's royalist troops and the parliamentary horse of Hesilrige's 'Lobsters'. Fairfax and his New Model Army were met by the Men of the Club on his way west, and though considering them royalist sympathisers (which was more true of the Wiltshire than the Dorset members) treated them with some respect. After his signal victory over Goring at Langport (Somerset), however, he turned with irritation on the clubmen and 'bloodily dispersed' them at Hambledon Hill (Dorset). They had little further effect.

After the capture of Bristol by Fairfax, royalist garrisons at Devizes, Lacock and Longford surrendered to Cromwell and the war in Wiltshire ground slowly to an end. January of 1646 saw a few raids from Oxford and Marlborough was briefly in royalist hands, but by June Lord Hertford surrendered Oxford, and Wiltshire forces on both sides were set free.

The Interregnum

At the war's conclusion no royalists were executed as war-criminals and only one in Wiltshire was wholly dispossessed. This was Francis, Baron Cottington, a former Chancellor of the Exchequer, who lost his Fonthill estate. But penalties were inflicted later on all the prominent royalists. The Seymour brothers, James Thynne of Longleat, the Earl of Danby, Sir William Button and Thomas Benett of Pythouse, Tisbury, paid a 'decimation' tax for their assumed support of a later revolt against parliament, which totalled nearly £40,000.

When Charles I was condemned to death by parliament in 1649 two prominent Wiltshire men, Edmund Ludlow and Sir John Danvers, were 'regicides', that is they signed his death warrant.

While the young Charles II escaped through Wiltshire after his disastrous defeat at Worcester in 1651, the county suffered no harm in the 'second Civil War' which had thus ended. In 1654, however, there was increasing intrigue by royal supporters and in the following year an ill-prepared rising took place. It had been planned, if that is the right word, to co-ordinate risings throughout the country in March, but only Colonel Penruddock of Compton Chamberlayne was prepared. With Sir Joseph Wagstaff, a 'soldier of fortune', he marched on Salisbury, seized assize judges and the sheriff and released royalist prisoners; Wagstaff favoured hanging the judges but Penruddock objected. Neither got the popular support they had expected and with an ever-diminishing troop rode westward in search of it, eventually surrendering at South Molton (Devon). Penruddock was hung at Exeter in the following spring.

The Commonwealth created by Cromwell as the substitute for royal government made itself increasingly unpopular as it fell into the hands of Puritanical extremists and as taxation increased. It was still more unpopular when Cromwell delegated regional government to the arbitrary hands of the 'major-generals'. But after the collapse of the Penruddock 'rebellion' and the imposition of the 'decimation' fines on royalists there were only minor troubles in the county, though these included the mutiny in 1659 of four troops of cavalry at Warminster who demanded a representative parliament. Such a move was repugnant to Edmund Ludlow, now an inflexible champion of extreme republican government, and he was driven into exile where he wrote his own account of the

Signatures of the two Wiltshire regicides, Sir John Danvers of Dauntsey and Sir Edmund Ludlow of Maiden Bradley, from the warrant for the execution of King Charles I, 1649. Danvers (1558-1655), was M.P. for Malmesbury, 1645, and member of the Council of State, 1649-53. Ludlow (1617-1692), M.P. for Wiltshire, 1646, and member of the Council of State, 1649 and 1650, died in exile in Vevey, Switzerland

Colonel John Penruddock of Compton Chamberlayne (1619-55)

77

Edward Hyde, 1st Earl of Clarendon (1609-74). Born at Dinton

Civil War. Following further quarrels between an unrepresentative parliament (the remaining members of the original Long Parliament elected in 1641) and a tired army, Charles II was, by popular consent, restored to the English throne in 1660.

Post-Restoration Wiltshire

Wiltshire's Edward Hyde, who had been Charles's chancellor in exile, was made a baron on the Restoration and Earl of Clarendon in the following year. The Hydes became the most important family in the county for the Seymours were still suffering from their losses in the Civil War and the Interregnum, while the Herberts of Wilton, who had supported Parliament even if half-heartedly, were out of favour and in decline even when the fame of Wilton House, its art treasures and its new gardens was growing. Clarendon gained considerably more influence when his daughter Anne married the new king's brother, later James II, while their daughter Mary married William of Orange and became queen of England in her own right. But the new opulence offended the royalists who had been impoverished by the late wars and his association with the so-called 'Clarendon Code', which attempted among other things to restore Anglican conformity, offended liberals and Nonconformists. Following disasters during the war with Holland, in 1667 he was forced into exile where he wrote his weighty *History of the Great Rebellion*. He never returned. At the succession of James II in 1685 Clarendon's two sons were now brothers-in-law to the king. Edward, now Lord Clarendon, was made Lord Privy Seal and his brother, Lord Rochester, was made Lord Treasurer.

Wiltshire remained almost immune from the ill-effects of the ill-managed rebellion in 1686 by the Protestant and favourite but illegitimate son of Charles II, the Duke of Monmouth, against the arbitrary rule and Catholic leanings of his uncle James. There were minor disturbances around Warminster, where Monmouth had expected support from the Thynnes of Longleat, but they were suppressed by the militia under the Earl of Pembroke and potential rebels were overawed by the royal army moving west. Two of the Longleat staff joined Monmouth's forces, however, and while the Wiltshire militia was attached to the royal army as it moved into Somerset, it was not thought reliable and was kept in reserve at the battle of Sedgemoor where Monmouth was routed. Two Wiltshire militiamen died in accidents. Six Wiltshiremen were whipped at Salisbury for seditious utterings and 16 Wiltshire rebels were sent to Wells for trial, but Wiltshire escaped the horrors of the Dorset and Somerset assizes. The Thynnes were upset only by the damage to the hay crop on their Somerset estate.

Catholic bias by the king in the appointment of army officers, however, dispersed the county's goodwill. In 1686 both the Hyde brothers were 'sacked' and the Catholic Lord Arundell of Wardour was made Lord Privy Seal. The king's attempts to remove all the local dignitaries were

Seth Ward (1617-89), Bishop of Salisbury 1667-89

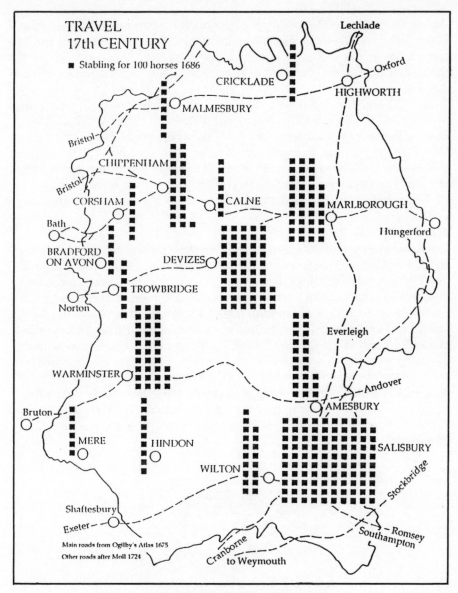

Map 10.

only cancelled by fear of the imminent invasion by his son-in-law William of Orange. William, however, landed successfully at Torbay in November 1688 (when he had been expected to land in Kent) and moved cautiously eastward, reaching Wiltshire in December. By then the royal army assembled by James at Salisbury had melted away. John Churchill (later Duke of Marlborough) was one of the deserters and is thought by many to have planned to hand over the king to William if the former had moved forward to Warminster, but instead James fled to London.

Lord Clarendon, who was dismayed at the desertion of James by members of his own family, then went forward to meet William. They met at Berwick St Leonard, home of his widowed mother. The other Wiltshire peers, Ailesbury (a relative of the Seymours), Pembroke, Weymouth (Thomas Thynne) and Clarendon's brother Rochester, remained cautiously in London but, when James fled from London on 11 December, joined in inviting William to take over the government.

Monuments

Great monuments of the Stuart era are few in the county, but they include in Wilton House one of the best in Britain. 'King Charles I did love Wilton above all places' (said Aubrey) and encouraged Lord Pembroke in his building, gardening and decoration. A house twice the size of the present was planned by Inigo Jones and Isaac de Caus about 1633, but Pembroke fell out of favour and was sacked from the position of Lord Chamberlain in 1640. Only half the original design was built following this, but it included in the 'Double Cube' room, designed as a setting for family portraits by Van Dyke, the most beautiful room of its time. The other great houses of that age, Amesbury Abbey, Fonthill Splendens and the rebuilt house of the Seymours at Wolf Hall near Bedwyn, have since been lost. Only one small church was built, at Standlynch.

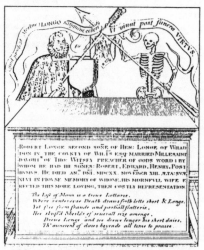

Monument to Robert Longe, died 1620,
Broughton Gifford church

28.   The Old Meeting House, Horningsham, which has a date-stone marked '1566' and is claimed to be the oldest Nonconformist chapel in the country. It was founded for Scottish Presbyterian workers at Longleat. The present building was mainly built about 1690.

29.   The Town Hall, Wootton Bassett, given by Laurence Hyde, 1st Earl of Rochester, in 1700. Hyde had been elected M.P. for the town in 1679. The building was restored by Lady Meux of Vastern in 1889.

30. Goddard memorial, Ogbourne St Andrew. The Goddards were large landowners in north Wiltshire and lords of the Manor of Swindon from the 16th to the 20th centuries.

31. The Matrons' College, Salisbury, founded in 1682 by Bishop Seth Ward, for the widows of clerics.

32. The Parade, Trowbridge. Eighteenth-century cloth merchants' houses (now brewery offices) in Wiltshire's county town.

33. Melksham Spa. Three-storeyed houses built for the early 19th-century spa. At the rear was the spring, pump house and baths.

34. Stourton parish church of St Peter, the small medieval church made picturesque by Sir Richard Colt Hoare to integrate it further into the design of the Stourhead Gardens. The gardens, the greatest achievement of the 18th-century English Landscape movement, were created by his grandfather, Henry Hoare II, the banker.

35.   Castle Combe. The view of this late-medieval cloth manufacturing town from the bridge over the By Brook.

VIII Georgian Wiltshire

During the mid-17th century the county had been a battleground. Its industry had been disrupted and its population had stagnated for much of the succeeding period. But at the end of the century the population rose sharply. No accurate figures exist but it has been reasonably estimated from the Protestation Returns of 1642 and Compton Census of 1676 that the population in the middle of the 17th century was about 113,500, and that one hundred years later, in the mid-18th century, it is thought to have risen to a hundred and fifty-seven thousand. By the end of the 18th century (and the figure is based on the first national census of 1801, corrected for the crudest errors) the population had reached nearly a hundred and eighty-four thousand. In the national context the county's growth had kept pace with the nation's throughout the 17th century, but during the 18th, while following similar trends of slower growth at the beginning and faster at the end, it lost ground relative to the rest of the country.

Design for a pumphead at Holt, 1731

Inside the county, Salisbury, its most important town, stagnated for more than a century and its population only reached 8,000 by 1801, which represented an addition of less than one fifth in 150 years. There was continuous emigration from the more rural areas, most of the migrants going to the manufacturing towns and villages of Western Wiltshire, where sharp rises in population enabled the county to keep pace, in population density, with neighbouring counties. In wealth too it kept pace with its neighbours. The general assessment of 1707 estimated its taxable wealth at £38 per square mile, as high as its industrial neighbour Gloucestershire, higher than Dorset and Hampshire, and only a little less than Somerset, though considerably below that of the Home Counties such as Berkshire at £58 and Surrey at £89. But the uneven growth of population, losses from the more rural areas and rapid growth in the manufacturing areas, led by the end of the century and for most of the 19th to the familiar problems of regional unemployment, poverty and overcrowding.

Government

The revolutions of the 17th century had brought new men to the top and new blood into the county. Thomas Pitt for instance, a wealthy East India merchant, bought most of the burgess plots at Old Salisbury and the neighbouring Stratford sub Castle, and so controlled the election of the M.P. for this now 'rotten' borough. His famous grandson, later Earl

The arms of the Methuen family

of Chatham, was its M.P. in 1734. The Bouveries, who had been foreign immigrants in Elizabeth's reign, had replaced the Gorges family at Longford Castle and, having consolidated their influence there, controlled the election of M.P.s in southern Wiltshire for many years. The more successful of the 17th-century clothiers had become gentry and used their estates to exercise political muscle in the north-west of the county. John Methuen, of the former clothing family of Bradford, had become Lord Chancellor of Ireland and achieved immortality by making the 'Methuen' or 'Port Wine' treaty with Portugal in 1703.

The older-established families of How and Hyde (relatives of Lord Clarendon) dominated the two county parliamentary seats for some three decades before 1722, but were displaced by the families of Goddard (which had purchased monastic lands around Swindon) and of Long of Draycott Cerne.

The boroughs of Salisbury and Devizes continued to return local men as M.P.s, but in the other boroughs the proportion of candidates who were local men fell until the Reform Act of 1832, even though their choice and management could be in the hands of important county landlords such as the earls of Pembroke, of Wilton, and the Seymours and Ailesburys of Savernake. Management of elections could be an expensive business and certainly proved onerous and damaging to the Ailesburys in trying to control the Marlborough contests.

Below this level county government was managed by government-appointed magistrates and continued almost unchanged, though the quarter sessions became more peripatetic in a worthy effort to deal with business on a local basis. Unfortunately it caused some confusion when cases were adjourned to the next sessions, held elsewhere, and there were occasions where no justices appeared at the latter to hear them. Courts of Request to deal with petty debt were introduced in the reign of George III and greatly reduced the work of higher courts. Hundred constables continued to serve the courts as forced but unpaid labour, and were made responsible for the returns of the first national census of 1801, a fact that accounts for much of its inaccuracy.

The new post of county surveyor was created to ensure that bridges designated as of some importance were kept in repair – it had previously been the duty of adjoining parishes and they were only too often in default – and this led to a better standard of bridge maintenance. The extensive improvement of the roads came late in the century.

Manorial courts continued to decline, particularly in the Cheese Country, and growing numbers were held only when the lord's agent could show that there was profit to be had from the fines of tenants. Business was often conducted by the agent writing out the draft agreements and getting any available labourer to witness them. Nevertheless there were instances, especially in the Chalk Country, where a full meeting of tenants was useful in settling the management of lands held in common. One court, at Great Cheverell south of Devizes, survived until 1908.

Church and education

The Established Church was in some disarray after the revolutions of the 16th and 17th century and, in spite of efforts of such post-Restoration bishops of Salisbury as Gilbert Burnet (1689-1715), settled down to a somnolent but reasonably tolerant life. At one extreme of the religious spectrum, Dissenters were now well established in West Wiltshire and were building their own churches. At the other were some Anglican ministers' families, and it became increasingly difficult to get young after they had sworn it to James II. Seven Anglican ministers were lost from this cause, but the majority accepted the Revolution easily and Bishop Burnet treated his lost clerics with kindness.

While many clergymen lived in handsome houses, those of the 18th century were built not from parish funds but from the resources of the ministers' families, and it became harder and harder to get young ministers to take on rural and impoverished parishes. Out of the 290 parishes, about a hundred and ten had lost their great tithes to outsiders, usually laymen like the Thynnes of Longleat, so that incumbents struggled to obtain the remaining lesser tithes from parishioners who were hostile to tithes and often in addition to the Established Church itself. The Church was much criticised then and later for non-residence and for pluralism among its clergy, and there was much to be criticised. Nearly half the incumbents in the county were not resident in their parishes and some were resident only in the summer months and retired, like the vicar of Longbridge, to more congenial places for the winter. And some justified their living far from their parish by their desire to get large families well educated. None of this is surprising but it had increasingly bad effects.

The first 'visitation' by Bishop Barrington revealed the state of each parish in 1783. The catechism of children was not even attempted in 30 per cent of the parishes because the children did not come to church and in any case could not read, while in half of all the parishes no schooling of any kind was available. This reflects on the indifference of both the Church and the landlords and was a state of affairs not remedied until the early 19th century, when first the Dissenters and then the Established Church (in self-defence) founded free schools.

There were of course some schools. Salisbury Cathedral had long had its own school and three other free schools had been founded by bequests in the 16th and 17th centuries: Dauntsey's at Lavington in 1542, Marlborough Grammar in 1550 (partly with monastic property) and Bentley's at Calne in 1664. One great landowner, Lord Weymouth of Longleat, founded another at Warminster in 1707, modelled on the early schools at Stanwell and Harrow (Middlesex), with a residence for

The arms of Marlborough College, 'Virtute, Studio, Ludo'

83

the headmaster in the centre of its rectangular block, decorated with an unwanted doorcase from Longleat.

Dissenters built a number of important chapels, notably the Quaker chapels at Corsham and Melksham and the Presbyterian edifices at Horningsham (which claims to be the oldest in the country) and Crockerton; the Established Church built only two new churches, of which only the severely classical church of 1779 at Hardenhuish, built by John Wood the younger of Bath for David Ricardo's in-laws, has survived.

Farming

The introduction of water meadows in the mid-17th century had now produced its own revolution in the chalk valleys and their adjoining arable fields, greatly increasing the amount of stock which could be maintained there, but there was a further decline in the number of family farms so that in the early 18th century less than half the farmland was in such hands. The difference between the Chalk and Cheese Countries was still widening for in the Cheese (and the Butter) areas small family farms could be buttressed by the labour of part-time craftsmen and traders. There the trends were to dispersal of land and to subsistence farming. In the corn and sheep areas the reverse was true. There most of the farms were market-oriented already, and the families and part-time farmers who had occupied nearly a third of them in the mid-17th century had been reduced to very few by the early eighteenth. Manorial management was still widespread here and ownership was being concentrated in a new breed of gentlemen-farmers, like the Tulls of Shalbourne (Jethro Tull was internationally famous for his pioneer methods), who did much to improve husbandry by example and education.

Farm rents, which had been relatively depressed from the mid-17th century to the mid-18th, started to rise sharply so that by the end of the century and particularly with the stimulus of the French wars the average was some five times above its mid-century figure. The income of the large landowners was thereby enormously increased. The prices of farm products, however, rose slowly and were at the end only double the figure at mid-century. Relatively depressed prices coupled with faster-rising rents further exacerbated the loss of family farms. Meanwhile the introduction of the spinning jenny into the cloth industry and its use in the new town-based factories took away the simple hand and wheel spinning which had been done by women and girls on hundreds of farms. The loss of this source of 'pin-money' was hard enough on the small Cheese Country farms: it was the last straw that broke the economy of family farms in the Chalk Country.

The inclosure of formerly common-fields added to the flight from the land. But even at the end of the 18th century, Board of Agriculture surveyors with a jaundiced view of common-fields and subsistence farming identified huge areas which they classified as 'waste', putting the figure for Wiltshire as high as 23 per cent, more than any southern

The interior of the octagon, Fonthill Abbey

The exterior of the octagon

84

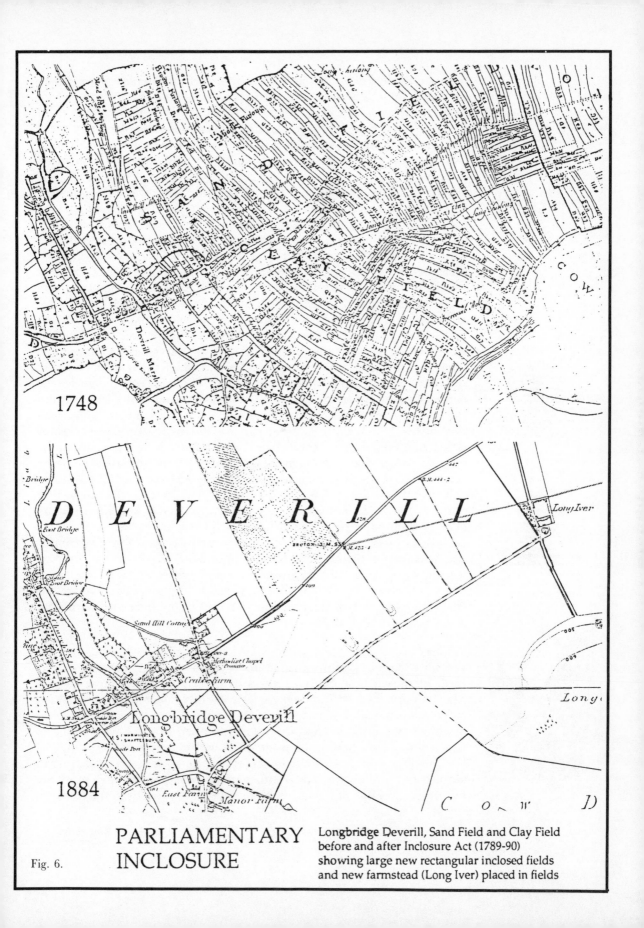

1748

1884

PARLIAMENTARY
INCLOSURE

Fig. 6.

Longbridge Deverill, Sand Field and Clay Field
before and after Inclosure Act (1789-90)
showing large new rectangular inclosed fields
and new farmstead (Long Iver) placed in fields

county outside Cornwall (figures for Somerset and Berkshire were nine per cent, for Gloucestershire three per cent, and Hampshire, which included most of the New Forest, 18 per cent). Wiltshire's figure must have included most of the remaining unenclosed land, for huge areas had already been enclosed. Most of the Cheese and Butter countries had long been fenced and hedged and exhibited a landscape not so different from today's.

There is little recorded of early enclosures. The earliest documented agreement to survive is dated 1632 and covers 1,806 acres of marshy ground at Hannington, which it was intended to drain and improve. Other early examples are also in the northern Cheese Country like the 986 acres at Highworth in 1749. Most of the Chalk Country was enclosed more sweepingly by parliamentary acts at the end of the century, at Chicklade in 1781, Warminster and Corsley in 1783 and Heytesbury in 1785, for example. Nearly seventy such acts were passed before 1800 and another 140 were passed before 1870, by when there was little left to enclose. In all this the smallholders lost much, and the landless labourers all, of their claim to fuel and pasture, but most landowners and improvers thought that the commons around which the poor struggled to survive had made them 'shiftless and idle'. Thomas Davis however, the perceptive steward of the Longleat estate at the end of the 18th century (he wrote an excellent treatise for the Board of Agriculture on farming in Wiltshire), showed some sympathy for the losses of the poor, for his estate had inherited a special problem, which it had permitted by inaction rather than intent, in the growth of a large squatter colony on common land south of Warminster. On the edge of this area of furze and rough grazing a few cottages had been built in the early 18th century. By 1781 nearly two hundred rough hovels had been put up along a little polluted stream which provided drinking water for 1,015 inhabitants, who now comprised a quarter of the population of Warminster. Attempts by the estate to legalise these squatters when the common was enclosed under the Warminster and Corsley act were met with suspicion, and they thereby lost all claims to compensation for the enclosure. The settlement remained a haunt of the poor and unruly for many years after.

Textiles

Wiltshire clothiers concentrated more than ever in west Wiltshire. Little cloth was now made in the outlying centres of Malmesbury and Marlborough, or at Wilton, where weavers had taken up the specialised carpet trade assisted by the earls of Pembroke. Clothiers now specialised in lighter 'medleys' or 'Spanish' cloths, made from fine wool much of which came from Spain, for production had outstripped the supply of fine English wools. The chief market was now at home rather than abroad and while export was still nationally important and probably five times the value of the other major exports put together, the clothiers

Malmesbury

86

were less dependent on the Merchant Venturers of Blackwell Hall in London, whose trade with northern Europe was interrupted so often by war. They were using instead the younger Levant Company which traded with the Mediterranean and the Near East, and they were also exporting direct to the American colonies. Even modest clothiers like the Wanseys of Warminster were learning to export directly. The Wanseys even accepted payment in West Indian sugar for some of their cloth, and might have made a fortune in the West Indies if it had not been for their distaste for slavery.

As these moves succeeded, complaints from clothiers about unfair competition became less, but those from merchants about the quality of medleys grew to such an extent that in 1727 the Government appointed medley inspectors for nine areas of the county, viz.: Trowbridge, Wingfield and North Bradley; Bradford on Avon; Crockerton and Horningsham; Boyton and Norton Bavant; Westbury; Melksham, Seend and South Newton; Bremhill and Chippenham; Lacock and Corsham; and Kingswood (now in Gloucs.). These areas show the distribution of the medley clothiers, but few records survive; the scheme did not work well and was soon forgotten. Salisbury's cloth industry was not included. It had been in relative decline for some time but had a resurgence in the 18th century by concentrating on finer cloths.

The clothiers had their ups and downs and many of the western ones did very well, as can be seen in the fine town houses designed by Bath architects in Bradford, Trowbridge, Chippenham and even Warminster, and from other grand houses in such villages as Seend and Steeple Ashton. Workers in the industry had more downs than their masters. There were riots during most of the frequent depressions in the industry as clothiers tried to relieve overheads by reducing wages. In 1726 there were serious riots at Bradford, Trowbridge and Melksham, when a man was killed by troops firing on an angry mob. But the rioters were exonerated at the subsequent inquiry, as local justices thought there were good grounds for grievance. This conciliatory attitude was unique in 18th-century industrial relations and after further riots in 1738 at Trowbridge and Melksham over similar grievances three of the ringleaders were hung.

Machinery to speed production in spinning, carding and weaving was introduced in the second half of the century and led to more trouble. The first spinning jenny in the West was introduced at Shepton Mallet (Somerset) in 1776. It was perceived as an immediate threat by workers in Somerset and Wiltshire and workers from Warminster joined in a riot there. But nevertheless its use spread rapidly and by 1783 there were petitions against it submitted by landowners and parish officers (mostly from rural areas) who complained it was causing widespread unemployment and overloading local poor rates.

The introduction of a power-driven shearing machine at Horningsham

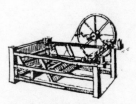

The spinning jenny

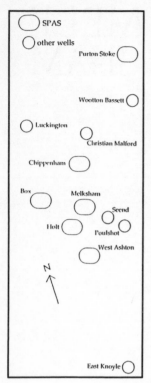

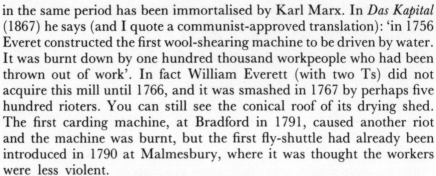

SPAS

other wells

Purton Stoke

Wootton Bassett

Luckington

Christian Malford

Chippenham

Box

Melksham

Seend

Holt

Poulshot

West Ashton

N

East Knoyle

Spas and other medicinal wells in Wiltshire

in the same period has been immortalised by Karl Marx. In *Das Kapital* (1867) he says (and I quote a communist-approved translation): 'in 1756 Everet constructed the first wool-shearing machine to be driven by water. It was burnt down by one hundred thousand workpeople who had been thrown out of work'. In fact William Everett (with two Ts) did not acquire this mill until 1766, and it was smashed in 1767 by perhaps five hundred rioters. You can still see the conical roof of its drying shed. The first carding machine, at Bradford in 1791, caused another riot and the machine was burnt, but the first fly-shuttle had already been introduced in 1790 at Malmesbury, where it was thought the workers were less violent.

While wages were low clothiers were loth to introduce expensive machinery, and it was not until increased competition from the fast-rising Yorkshire industry, where machinery had been accepted, that the Wiltshire clothiers pressed ahead with their own. Failure to modernise has been seen as the cause of the total loss of the Wiltshire industry by the mid-20th century, but while Wiltshire lost some of its early advantages in the 18th century due to bad industrial relations, it did not fail to modernise in the nineteenth. Meanwhile not only the better clothiers but still more the great landowners had become very rich and all were anxious to improve their houses, parks and life-styles.

Improvements

Major roads were being improved to the spa at Bath, the 'resort of the sound rather than the sick' as Defoe put it. The population of Bath grew from only 2,000 in 1700 to 34,000 by the end of the century, far outstripping any Wiltshire town, and the first toll-roads (the 'turnpikes') were made on routes to the city. The success of Bath's spa had an effect on north-west Wiltshire comparable to the spread of villas into Wiltshire from the Roman city, and led also to its imitation where there were other springs of possible medical interest. Soon there were spas at Seend, where the waters had been recommended by Aubrey in 1684, at Middlehill (Box) and Holt. None were successful for long. At Holt only an elaborately framed pump remains, and efforts in the 19th century to create new spas at Melksham and Purton Stoke were also failures.

Bath satsified the needs of those who could find little entertainment in Wiltshire towns, though many of the county's inns built 'assembly rooms' for their winter seasons, but the display of houses and gardens at Bath and notably Ralph Allen's Prior Park, made most of Wiltshire's seem dowdy and unfashionable. The 18th century therefore saw a surge in building and landscaping unparalleled since late-Elizabethan days. Longleat and Wilton already had extravagant gardens but they were altered to suit the new fashions. The Bolingbrokes rebuilt their house at Lydiard Tregoze, the Seymours rebuilt their house at Marlborough (now the nucleus of the College), the Earl of Suffolk modernised his

The London to Bath mail-coach, 1784

88

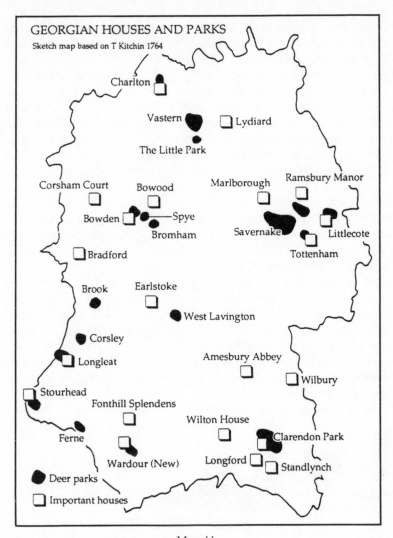

GEORGIAN HOUSES AND PARKS

Sketch map based on T Kitchin 1764

Charlton

Vastern
Lydiard

The Little Park

Corsham Court
Bowood
Marlborough
Ramsbury Manor

Bowden
Spye

Bromham
Savernake
Littlecote

Bradford
Tottenham

Brook
Earlstoke

West Lavington

Corsley

Amesbury Abbey

Longleat
Wilbury

Stourhead

Fonthill Splendens

Wilton House

Ferne
Clarendon Park

Wardour (New)
Longford
Standlynch

Deer parks

Important houses

Map 11.

house at Charlton Park and the Earls of Shelburne rebuilt and extended
Bowood House twice in the century. Corsham Court was rebuilt by the
Methuens and filled, like Wilton, with works of árt, and the Arundells
of Wardour built the largest Georgian house in the county one mile
from their ruined castle, which they preserved as a romantic feature
complete with a grotto from a grotto specialist at Tisbury. In Savernake
Forest, where the Seymours' interest had passed to their relatives the
Bruce (later Brudenell-Bruce) family, the latter converted the estate
into part farmland and part commercial forestry, but planted enormous
avenues of beech focussed on the hunting lodge of Tottenham which
replaced the decayed Wolf Hall of the Seymours. Aubrey had described

89

The Temple of Apollo, Stourhead gardens, erected in 1765

the lodge as a 'pile of good architecture' but the house was rebuilt in the 1720s in grand and Palladian fashion (only to be rebuilt again at vast expense in 1825).

In addition to these houses two of the most extravagant displays in the country were made by City merchants in the south of the county. The Hoares at Stourhead built a new house near the site of Lord Stourton's decayed home, and then a series of great lakes, waterfalls, a grotto, bridges and temples, together with 2,000 acres of trees, to produce a landscape akin to a Claude Lorraine painting. It is now one of the finest gardens in the world. At Fonthill the Beckfords, not content with their 'Splendens' house and lake, produced a gigantic mock-Gothic 'abbey'. It was started 'at a monstrous rate' in 1796 but never completed, though work included large plantations, a lake and a 12-foot wall around its extensive park. It was used to entertain Nelson for three spectacular nights in 1800, and abandoned by the younger Beckford in 1823. It collapsed in ruins in 1825.

Much landscaping was done by gifted amateurs like the Hoares but more was done by the great professionals of the age and their work was imitated by lesser men. William Kent (1685-1748) was employed at Wilton, Lancelot Brown (1715-83) at Longleat, Bowood, Tottenham House and Longford Castle, and when fashions changed Humphry Repton was called in at Longleat, Corsham and Bowood to 'modernise' the landscape. In addition at Stourhead and at Erlestoke parts of the village were incorporated as romantic objects in the estate's landscape.

These are the great monuments of the Georgian Age in Wiltshire.

The Grammar School in the Close, Salisbury

IX The Agricultural 'Revelation' and the New Poor Law

Sellar and Yeatman in that memorable history of England *1066 and All That* observe that simultaneously with the Industrial Revolution 'there was an Agricultural Revelation which was caused by the invention of turnips'. This may have been a fair summary for the eastern counties of England, but in Wiltshire introduction of turnips actually helped to destroy the subtle balance of sheep, corn and water-meadows on the thinner (i.e. most of the chalk) soils of the county. As in Ireland the poor were only saved by the 'invention' of the potato.

The Wiltshire Drill, by Reeves of Bratton

Throughout the 19th century Wiltshire was one of the poorest counties in England and sometimes the worst-off. In 1846-7 for instance one sixth of the total population was given poor relief. In spite of the need of the growing population for food and demands created by the French wars, life for the smaller tenant farmers and farm-labourers was hard and particularly so on the chalklands which occupy so much of the county.

Nevertheless high prices for farm products, which were sustained for the first decade of the century, inspired many landowners to farm improvement. The Earl of Suffolk and Berkshire at Charlton in north-west Wiltshire introduced and subsidised Scottish farmers to work on his somewhat backward estate. Farming societies became popular throughout the county once the success of the oldest, the Bath and West Agricultural Society, founded in 1774, was recognised. In 1813 the South West Wiltshire Farming Society and the Wiltshire Society for the Improvement of Agriculture were founded. Following these many groups were formed, usually for testing new machinery, but some with a more philosophical bent like the South Wiltshire and Warminster Farmers' Club, which was debating in 1843 whether it was proper to employ women treading soil to reduce wire-worm.

Life for the larger Wiltshire farmers, as opposed to their labourers, was not always so gloomy. Inclosure by Act of Parliament, designed to increase production, continued well into the 19th century. The greatest number of such schemes were approved in the first two decades of the century and further acts were passed, though in declining numbers, down to 1869. But in spite of these inclosures Salisbury Plain was still largely unsheltered and unfenced in the mid-century. Sheep increased in number throughout the county, by about six per cent in the first three decades and another ten per cent in the following two and a half. Six hundred thousand were supported by the Plain alone. Most of them were kept primarily for their manure value because the sale of the wool from the Wiltshire Horned sheep had now become negligible, while the breed itself had been slowly displaced by sheep of the South Down type, which were not immediately adaptable to the difficult farming conditions of the area or to the prevalent demands of the market. Nevertheless the increased numbers of sheep did for some time support the increased arable acreage provided by the ploughing of downland on the valley fringes, and Wiltshire grain growers, like farmers throughout most of the country, profited when the Crimean War cut off Russian grain imports.

Not all improvement was successful and at the beginning of the century Thomas Davis warned against haste in attempting improvements. He was particularly anxious about the ploughing of the downlands. The Ailesbury estate at Tottenham in Savernake found itself in considerable difficulties from its own extravagance. The family not only rebuilt its late-18th-century home in a grander manner in the 1820s, but expended large sums in bribes to electors to maintain their control of the adjoining parliamentary boroughs and at the same time indulged in ill-considered farm-building improvements which impressed their visitors but did little to raise the efficiency of their farms. The Pembroke estate, however, which was the largest in Wiltshire, was consistent, progressive and successful in balancing the improvement of buildings and farming methods, and with their profits were able to build a model farm at Quidhampton with Italianate cloisters (supposed to resemble a Russian dacha). More cautious investment was made by the Marquis of Bath in his larger estate based on Longleat (much of which lay in Somerset and elsewhere), particularly under the management of his best known stewards, Thomas Davis, father and son.

The Corn Laws, first introduced in 1815 and intended to restore farmers' prosperity after the fall of prices as the Napoleonic wars ended by a mixture of subsidies and import duties, divided opinion in the county. After massive demonstrations in the industrial areas they were repealed in 1846. Neither the laws nor the repeal had the full effect that interested parties claimed. The acts had given some security to the larger farmers but had done little for the smaller ones and nothing for the farm labourers. Nor was there the expected slump in corn production in Wiltshire following the repeal of the laws and the import of cheaper grain from Russia and Egypt, then from Australia and lastly from new lands in America. Grain prices were kept high by the demands of the rapidly growing population elsewhere in the country, but this led to an over-extension of grain output in the county which proved unremunerative as well as exhausting the chalk soils. In 1800 arable land occupied about one fifth of the county's land. In 1870 one third was under corn alone.

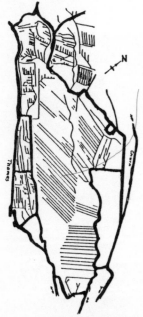

Drainage channels of former water meadows between the Rivers Thames and Churn at Cricklade

The expansion of arable farming was followed by an intense agricultural depression beginning in 1879-80, which the corn-growers blamed on foreign imports. The effects of the depression were exacerbated locally by failure of the new breeds of sheep to provide the expected return from wool. The Pembroke estates, which had continued their policy of improvement and been the first to introduce shelter belts on the downland, came off comparatively lightly from this depression, but elsewhere there were lasting effects on the chalkland farms from which they hardly recovered until after the Second World War. There was a rapid change in land use: between 1870 and 1910 the area of arable land in the county fell by 30 per cent, and nearly all of this reverted by neglect to permanent pasture. The eminent agronomist Sir Daniel Hall talked then of the 'quiet prosperity among the farmers' on the Wiltshire downs, but his was a view which would have been shared by few working in the area. Soon some would be making more money from rabbits than crops. The water meadows which had been the mainstay of the downland system decayed because their labour-intensive upkeep had become too costly and artificial fertilisers and new grasses provided alternatives. Traces of the meadows can be found in the valleys of the Wylye and Avon, south of Salisbury. Attempts have been made to revive the system in the latter part of this century.

Richard Jefferies (1848-87), author of Wildlife in a Southern County, Bevis *and* The Story of my Heart, *and writer on rural affairs, born at Coate, near Swindon*

Riots

In these ups and downs, the Wiltshire farm labourer stayed down. In 1794 his weekly wage averaged 7s.; in 1805 it was 8s.; for a short time in 1814 it reached 12s. But 7s. in 1794 bought 14 loaves, the main item of peasant diet, while in 1814 12s. only bought nine. The poor state of the labourers was the subject of acid comment from William Cobbett when he rode from Salisbury to Warminster in 1826 and contrasted the beautiful state of farms and countryside with the lot of the labourers, saying it was 'not very easy for the eyes of man to discover a labouring people more miserable'.

There were food riots in 1795 and 1796, in 1800 and 1801 and again in 1810, 1811, 1812 and 1813, but these were more often in the towns than countryside, and were associated with protest against new machinery in the textile industries. The countryside did not become inflamed to the same degree until the introduction of threshing machines. For most farm workers winter was a time of unemployment when one of the few guaranteed jobs was the hand-threshing of corn, which could take up to three months, from September to December. Harvests in 1828, 1829 and 1830 were poor and the new threshing machines, while modest horse-operated equipment, not the giant, steam-driven threshers of the end of the century, appeared a symbol of unemployment and even starvation. Riots in country areas swept the south-east of England and were known collectively as the 'Swing Riots' after a fictitious 'Captain Swing' whose

Threatening letter delivered to a Wiltshire farmer:
'this is to inform you what you have to undergo Jentelmen if providing you Dont pull down your meshenes and rise the poor mens wages the maried men give tow and six pence a day a day [sic] the singel tow shilings or we will burn down your barns and you in them this is the last notis
from WHR

93

ADDRESS

TO THE

LABOURERS

OF

WILTS.

FELLOW COUNTRYMEN!

BEWARE of False Prophets! Beware of those who excite you to Riot and Tumult, under the pretence of improving your Lot! Will the destruction of *Corn* give you *Bread?* Will it not *increase* the *Price?* Don't you perceive that the object of the *Incendiaries* is *not* to do you good, but to promote confusion? Where you have Distresses to complain of, rest assured that the Farmers and Land-owners will do all in their Power to alleviate them, and will pay all attention to your wants. But the strong Hand of the Law *must* and *will* put down all illegal Proceedings.

ENGLISHMEN! beware of Traitors, who would expose you to all the Horrors of Civil War, which they would not have the courage to brave themselves, and who would sacrifice your welfare to their own views of ambition and aggrandisement! Prove to the Nation, that **WILTSHIRE FREEMEN ARE NOT TO BE DISGRACED** by listening to such Instigators; and then yours will be the proud reflection, that, in the midst of confusion, you have remained **TRUE TO YOUR KING, YOUR COUNTRY, and YOUR GOD!**

A WILTS LANDOWNER.

W. B. BRODIE AND CO., PRINTERS, SARUM.

Fig. 7. Address to the Labourers of Wiltshire during the Swing riots, 1830.

letters to land-owners threatened with destruction those introducing the new machines.

Riots started in Kent in August 1830. They swept north as far as Norfolk and west through Hampshire and Wiltshire and then into Dorset, Gloucestershire and Berkshire during the autumn and early winter. The first incidents in Wiltshire were in mid-November. There was arson at Amesbury, Everleigh and Winterslow by the 21st of the month. By the 23rd it is said that all the threshing machines in the Salisbury area had been smashed. Salisbury itself was attacked by a mob on the same day and and textile machinery at Wilton was destroyed. Rioting reached its climax in the Tisbury area on the 29th in spite of appeals for calm in the local paper: 'The times are bad but burning corn will not give you bread', and rewards offered for the apprehension of incendiaries. Here a mob, after smashing machinery at Hindon market, made for Pythouse, the home of John Benett, one of the county M.P.s, who 'had the misfortune to be extremely unpopular both with the farmers and the labourers'. The local militia was called from Salisbury and with drawn swords they rode down the protesters, many of whom were now drunk, and caused considerable injuries. One protester was shot through the head. The remainder were herded or, if wounded, carted to the gaol at Salisbury. At proceedings at Salisbury in the following January, John Benett was foreman of the Grand Jury. Three hundred and thirty-nine prisoners were tried; two were sentenced to death but later reprieved; 150 were sentenced to transportation.

Wiltshire lost more threshing machines than other counties but the damage to local farming was not severe. Threshing machines were not popular with small farmers, who were trying to keep up with the large by introducing them, while the the riot at Pythouse was unique in occurring in an area of exceptional poverty and at the expense of an unpopular landlord. Three-quarters of the labourers in this area were on poor-relief. The reintroduction of threshing machines was deferred for some years but otherwise the riots, which were essentially 'conservative', did the labourers little good. The average farm-labourer's weekly wage now fell below 8s. a week, and with those of Gloucestershire, Herefordshire, Somerset and Dorset became the lowest in the country by 1850.

The New Poor Law

Hardship among the country workers had been sharpened by a well-intentioned but ill-considered bureaucratic intervention known as the 'Speenhamland system' following a meeting of Berkshire magistrates at Speenhamland near Newbury in 1795. There the magistrates had decided to top up labourers' wages from the local poor rates whenever they fell below a certain level. The poor rates had been intended for the preceding three centuries solely to assist the 'impotent' poor, but the system devised by the Berkshire magistrates was taken up in adjoining counties and

The riot at Pythouse

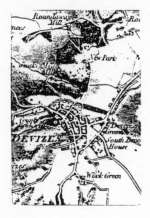

Devizes, Trowbridge and Melksham, three market and industrial towns, in 1817

soon resulted in a reduction in average wages and increases in local rates to make up the difference.

Apart from the inevitable distortion of the labour market the increased rate burden hit the small farmers, who employed few, if any, labourers, harder than it hit the large farmers. There were increasing demands for the cessation of this 'scandalous expenditure', which certainly rose sharply after the Napoleonic wars. In addition a drop in the morale of the labourers was noted by Thomas Davis and by Cobbett. Davis said 'indolence seems instinctive in the whole district' (of Southern Wiltshire) though he admitted it might be due, as it no doubt was, to malnutrition.

With the rising burden of the Old Poor Law rates and following the Swing riots of 1830, public opinion turned sharply against the poor. Ways of making the poor law more cost-effective were sought and following other government intervention in social reform, the Poor Law Amendment Act of 1834 (usually known as the 'New Poor Law') was devised and passed with speed and little opposition. Its chief authors were a Manchester economist, Edwin Chadwick, and Nassau Senior, son of the vicar of Durnford, Wiltshire. Both were Benthamites and could be described as liberal do-gooders.

Under the scheme devised in the new act no 'outdoor' relief was to be given to the able-bodied poor. If they needed relief they had to seek it in a workhouse. Relief there would have to be earned and would never exceed the wages of the independent labourer. To make the system uniform, which was a Benthamite principle, unions of parishes were to be set up and managed by boards of guardians consisting of the local Justices of the Peace with one elected representative of each of the union's parishes. Detailed guidance would be given by three commissioners in London, soon to be known as 'the three kings of Somerset House'. A central workhouse was to be provided for each union (hence the name 'Union' applied to the house itself) and its regime was to be harsh enough to deter all but the desperate from claiming relief. The arbitrary powers of the 'three kings' were taken over later by boards responsible directly to parliament and then by the Ministry of Health, but most of the system survived almost unchanged until 1930 and parts until 1948.

The new system had its teething troubles. At the Calne workhouse paupers tried to break into the strong-room, refusing to take bread in lieu of money, and they were still being given the five meat meals a week of the previous regime, which was much more than an independent labourer could expect. This was soon to be altered. By March 1835 the new Bradford on Avon and Calne unions had been formed. By November, 15 more were established. For most the energetic Assistant Commissioner Charles à Court of Heytesbury was responsible, and the size of individual unions varied according to the potential chairman thought suitable by à Court. The banker, Ravenhill, was found for the Warminster Union and the land-owner Ludlow Bruges for Melksham, but there were

96

36. The Palladian Bridge, Wilton House, 1737, designed by the 9th Earl of Pembroke and Roger Morris.

37. Bowood House, home of the Marquesses of Lansdowne: the Adam wing and the topmost of the 19th-century terraces. The 'Great House' was demolished in 1955.

38. Pythouse, the home of John Benett, built 1805. It was the scene of the large-scale agricultural labourers' riot in November 1830.

39.   Marlborough College incorporates the motte of the Norman castle and, in the present 'C' House, the 'new house' of the 6th Duke of Somerset, begun in 1699.

40.   Amesbury Abbey, the house built in the early 19th century by Thomas Hopper for Sir Edward Antrobus, owner of the Stonehenge estate. It replaced the house built in 1661 by John Webb for the Duke of Somerset.

41. A 'round house' originally protecting a horse engine, Manor Farm, Horningsham.

42. The farm buildings of the Wilton Estate's model farm at Quidhampton, built in the mid-19th century in Italianate style.

43. George Ford, the Stonehenge shepherd, *c*.1900.

44. Semington Hospital, former workhouse of the Trowbridge Union.

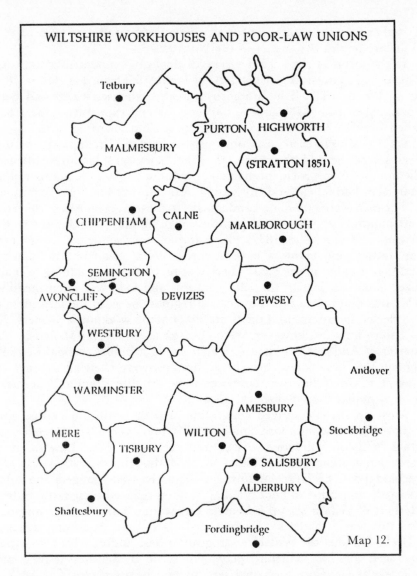

WILTSHIRE WORKHOUSES AND POOR-LAW UNIONS

Tetbury

MALMESBURY

PURTON   HIGHWORTH

(STRATTON 1851)

CHIPPENHAM   CALNE

MARLBOROUGH

SEMINGTON

AVONCLIFF

DEVIZES

PEWSEY

WESTBURY

Andover

WARMINSTER

AMESBURY

Stockbridge

MERE

WILTON

TISBURY

SALISBURY

ALDERBURY

Shaftesbury

Fordingbridge

Map 12.

difficulties at Marlborough and at Highworth because of jealousy of Swindon, and at Tisbury due to the awkwardness of John Benett of Pythouse.

The system was not welcome to some other interests. Trowbridge shopkeepers, for instance, complained of the loss of trade because paupers were no longer given cash. But eventually 328 parishes were formed into 26 unions, though three Wiltshire parishes were joined to unions centred outside the county, as Ludgershall was for many years to the infamous union of Andover (Hants.). Salisbury was left to itself, but only until 1869. By 1839, 13 new workhouses had been built, two others were under construction, and 10 older houses had been enlarged.

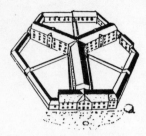

Warminster Union Workhouse, 1836, a reconstruction

Together they constituted as frightening an addition to the landscape of Wiltshire as did the castles of the Normans.

In the terms of the act's devisers all this was temporarily successful. The average poor-rate per head in the county fell from 14s. 6d. in 1833 to 8s. 9d. in 1837. The Bradford union workhouse, which had been upgraded to take 400 paupers, had only 95 and expenditure there had fallen from £200 to £61 a year. Charles à Court, writing to the 'three kings' in March 1836, was obviously delighted. Unemployment had been solved, he said, the character of the agricultural labourer stiffened, the number of improvident marriages reduced (in fact the number of all marriages had fallen) and cultivation 'was improved out of recognition'.

The poor were humiliated and abused in these workhouses by enforced and mindless activities and pointless regulations. John Parker in the Warminster house in 1837, for example, was sentenced to solitary confinement for having a pack of cards. Worst of all was the paucity and poor quality of the food. There was no Christmas pudding to make jokes about till late in the 19th century, and food was often inedible. This was due not so much to central regulations as to the meanness of the elected guardians and the brutality of many workhouse masters. No Wiltshire inmates, however, were cheated to the degree shown by the master of Andover workhouse, which led to a public scandal in 1842, though the 'best bones', which the inmates were chewing to stave off starvation when they were supposed to be grinding them to bone-meal, were supplied from Salisbury.

Most unions encouraged emigration of poor families overseas. Two hundred left Downton for Canada in 1836 and over 500 emigrated from other Wiltshire villages by 1842, but the use of Poor Law funds to assist emigration was forbidden in 1853 though emigration was still encouraged. The large landowners themselves encouraged and often assisted emigration of poor families: it often relieved their rates. Sidney Herbert of Wilton set up a Female Emigration Fund for this purpose, and this was a model for his brother-in-law, Lord Ailesbury, when in 1849 he founded the Wiltshire Emigration Association. This association arranged for 258 Wiltshire people to settle in South Australia and Victoria (away from the penal settlements) before it closed in 1852.

The unions were abolished in 1930 and the Poor Law was 'buried' (to quote Aneurin Bevan) in 1948, but some Wiltshire workhouses survive in whole or part. Those for Devizes, Melksham, Pewsey and Warminster are hospitals. That for Bradford on Avon, which is much older than the New Poor Law, has been converted into holiday flats.

X More Revolutions

Roads

Transport in and across Wiltshire was probably at its worst in the 17th century, for the old pack-horse routes which had served royal progressions and the trade of earlier centuries had now been cut to muddy pieces by increasingly-heavy wheeled traffic. This is amply testified by Samuel Pepys, Celia Fiennes and many other travellers of the period.

In 1668 Samuel Pepys travelled with his family from Oxford to Bath by way of Salisbury and Wilton. It was not of course a direct route but he was anxious to see Stonehenge, which was, as always, one of the great curiosities of the age. From Salisbury he had to hire guides to lead him to Stonehenge. Leaving Salisbury for Wilton he complained of the exorbitant charges of the inn and the cost of hiring horses, and when he left Wilton, without guides, he got lost on the Plain. As darkness fell he was lucky enough to stumble on an inn at Chitterne where the landlord smartly turned a pedlar out of a room to make space for Pepys's family.

In 1687 Celia Fiennes too travelled from Salisbury to Bath, but by coach. She did not get lost, but beyond Warminster her coach was soon stuck fast in sticky mud, from which it had to be lifted by a large party of men. As she commented, the way was only fit for packhorses 'which is the way of carriage in those parts'. But even half a century later Defoe would have been lost on the southern edge of Salisbury Plain if he had not met the many shepherds there who could direct him on his way.

The introduction of toll roads, the turnpikes, from the early 18th century, the improvement of rivers and then the construction of new waterways at the end of the century revolutionised transport throughout England, but the drive for these improvements came from outside this inland county, for example from the national postal system introduced by Ralph Allen of Bath. Wiltshire was to many traders and travellers simply a rural interlude in journeys between urbanised areas such as Bath and Bristol to the west and Reading and London to the east.

Prehistoric trading routes had radiated from Salisbury Plain but it, as described above, lost its central importance before the Roman invasion. The Roman road network was centred on the provincial capital at Cirencester north of the county and even the junction of the main road south with the west-to-east 'lead road' from the Mendips at Old Salisbury failed to create an important settlement or make Wiltshire a

Routes shown on the Gough Map

99

magnet for trade routes. When the Romans withdrew, the Saxon kings reverted to a more natural and modest pattern of routes, the 'herepaths', for the movement of the county militia, and these became the king's highways.

The mid-13th century map named after Gough shows a national network of roads radiating from London. Two of these crossed Wiltshire, a southern route through Winchester and Salisbury to Exeter and a northern one through Hungerford, Marlborough and Chippenham to Bristol. Both were important to Wiltshire's cloth industry down to the 19th century, but the northern route running to Bristol was even more important to the latter's traders, who often complained of obstructions on the Wiltshire section of the road. In 1281 a parson at Chippenham actually enclosed part of this road for his own use.

Ogilby's road atlas of 1675, the first of its kind, shows in considerable detail the older main roads to Bristol and to Exeter but also designates as important a road from London to Barnstaple which winds through Amesbury, Warminster and Maiden Bradley, and a number of cross-country routes, for example from Oxford to Bristol through Highworth and Malmesbury, from Marlborough to Norton St Philip (Somerset) through Devizes and Trowbridge, and from Salisbury to Lechlade (Gloucs.) through Marlborough and Highworth. It shows a branch from the Bristol road diverging at Chippenham to reach Bath via Bradford on Avon. A further road to Bath leaving the Bristol road and going more directly to Bath was not considered by Ogilby as important, although it was already in use by coaches from London to Bath and Bristol, and was soon to be known, as it is today, as 'the Bath Road'.

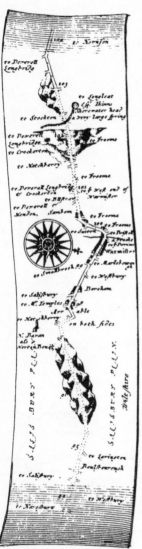

Part of the road from London to Barnstaple via Amesbury and Warminster, from John Ogilby's Britannia *(1675)*

Turnpikes

The first act for the construction of an improved toll-road for through traffic was passed in 1663, a few years before Ogilby's atlas. The first three acts for 'turnpikes' in Wiltshire were passed in 1706-7. They were all on the route to Bath and Bristol. Further turnpike acts covered roads radiating from the market towns of Salisbury, Devizes and Warminster, and created a network that covered the county by the 1760s. The Macadam family, of international fame, were surveyors or advisers for most of these new roads. On the Bath Road the turnpike trustees installed water pumps to lay dust by the mid-1750s, but most of the other new roads were simply improved chalk or gravel tracks. In the clay vales the general state of roads continued to be notoriously bad. As late as the 1830s Cobbett was finding his own way across Wiltshire, averse to paying tolls, but he found plenty of trouble on his way and was often lost.

The best use of the new roads was made by stage-coaches, and speed between towns improved notably, as we can tell from their timetables. The average speed of the run from London to Salisbury improved from

100

seven to ten miles per hour between 1771 and 1836, and a similar improvement was made between London and Devizes.

Canals

In the clay country of North Wiltshire there was little improvement in transport until the introduction of canals. The first of these, the Thames and Severn Canal, which crossed the northern tip of the county between Marston Meysey and Inglesham, was completed in 1789, long after many other canals outside Wiltshire. Of course Wiltshire did have two important rivers, the Bristol and the Salisbury Avons, and an early 'navigation' on the Salisbury Avon was made under an act of 1664 between Christchurch (now in Dorset) and Wylye. But due to difficulties with adjoining land and mill-owners on the river it was abandoned by 1730.

More important, and the most significant waterway improvement in the county's history, was the Kennet & Avon Canal, designed to connect Bristol and London. Again the impetus came from outside the county. The canal had been mooted since 1626 but was not begun until 1794 when it was spurred on by the necessities of the French wars. From the east it reached Bedwyn in 1799, but from the west it did not reach the steep incline west of Devizes until 1807. It was finally made navigable throughout when an impressive flight of locks, only surpassed in the canal system by a flight near Birmingham, was completed at Devizes in 1810.

The Bromham milestone on the Devizes-Chippenham turnpike

The less valuable Wiltshire & Berkshire Canal, branching from the Kennet & Avon near Semington, reached Wootton Bassett in 1801 and was completed to the Thames at Abingdon in 1810, while a branch to the Thames at Cricklade, called the North Wiltshire Canal, was added in 1819.

The success of all was assured for some decades by the opening in 1805 of the Somerset Coal Canal, for this halved the cost of coal to the west-Wiltshire factory towns and to other towns on its course like Devizes, as well as east as far as Reading. By the 1830s, which were the heydays of the canal, the Kennet & Avon was carrying nearly 350,000 tons of traffic a year, of which half was coal. Most of this came from the Somerset coalfield via the Somerset canal, but some also from the field north of Bristol which was connected to the Avon by a tram-road (as were the Bath stone quarries). At the same time the Wiltshire & Berkshire canal was carrying another 70,000 tons a year, of which over two-thirds was Somerset coal, to Swindon and other places in north Wiltshire and in Oxfordshire. In addition both canals carried 'Bath' stone from Box and Corsham and many items imported through the port of Bristol, such as Irish timber, Welsh slate and West Indian sugar. Of the local products transported by the canals wheat and barley formed the major part.

101

For these canals, which were a great stimulus to north Wiltshire's economy, the railway era arrived too soon and few canals paid their way, let alone any good return to the shareholders for their massive investment. The Kennet & Avon, for example, had built a broad canal (unlike the majority of English canals) 57 miles long, with 106 locks, of which 29 were in the two miles west of Devizes, handsome aqueducts,

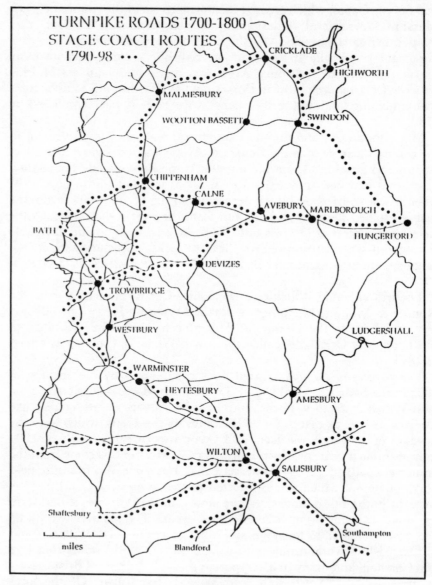

Map 13.

a tunnel, bridges and two pumping stations required to maintain suf-
ficient water in the canal's top level at Bedwyn.

Railways
Bristol merchants were the midwives of the Great Western Railway,
which transformed the economy of much of north Wiltshire for the

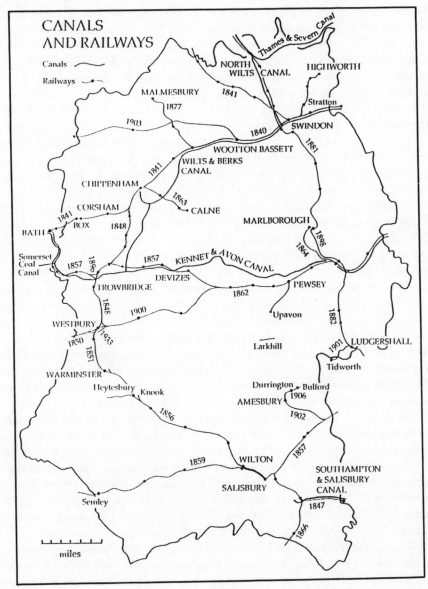

Map 14.

second time in 50 years. This railway company was formed in 1833 to link Bristol to London, hence the heraldic shields of both cities incorporated in its coat of arms, and its line was chosen by its young chief-engineer, I. K. Brunel, to run through the clay vales rather than the shorter but hillier route through the downland valleys. It was started with vigour from the London end, reached a point near Wootton Bassett in 1841, and was extended and opened to Bristol in the following year. In the same year (1842) a branch line to Gloucester and Cheltenham was started from a junction with the main line about two miles north-west of Old Swindon. In addition a new station with a hotel and restaurant was built at the junction, while workshops for the maintenance of the railway, halfway between its London and Bristol terminals, were started in 1843 on an adjoining site. Water was provided from the now-doomed Wiltshire & Berkshire Canal while stone for building the hotel, the workshops and a complete new village, 'New Swindon', with its own church and school, was brought from a vein of Box stone found when the two-mile tunnel under Box Hill was built. A minor curiosity, but probably not deliberately designed, is the fact that the sun can shine right through the Box tunnel on Brunel's birthday.

In 1848 the Wiltshire, Somerset & Weymouth Railway with the assistance of the G.W.R. built a line from Chippenham, on the Bristol line, to Westbury, and this was extended to Warminster in 1850. It was taken on to Salisbury's Fisherton Street in 1856, where the city had been joined to London (more or less) by the rival London & South Western Railway, whose line from Eastleigh reached Milford on the east side of the city in 1847. The L. & S.W.R. built a more direct route from London in 1857 which ran via Andover and the Winterbourne valley, and this line was extended by way of Fisherton Street and the Nadder valley to Yeovil in 1859. In the same year a short line was built from the 1857 Fisherton Station to the Market Hall in the centre of the city, while the Fisherton stations of the rival railway companies were rebuilt as a joint station. Salisbury was now blessed with three stations.

Other lines, including a major route from Andover to Marlborough, Swindon and eventually Cheltenham by the L. & S.W.R., soon formed a network over the county so that only the more remote chalk uplands were more than a few miles from a railway station. One minor line demonstrated some enterprise locally when the Harris family, bacon producers of Calne, raised the capital to build a link between Chippenham and Calne, which provided the Marquis of Lansdowne with a private halt where it crossed the Bowood estate.

The Great Western and its subsidiaries had, at Brunel's insistence, used a broad gauge for their lines. This was just over seven feet between rails instead of the 'standard' gauge of 4 foot 8½ inches adopted by all other companies. Increasing friction at points of contact led the Great Western to accept the standard gauge and consequently their tracks

North Star, a steam engine of the 1830s, from a replica in the Swindon railway museum

were converted between 1872 and 1875, with impressive speed on great sections of the line.

The growing demand for fresh milk by the London market led to its exploitation by the railways. Wholesale milk depots were set up at Semley on the L. & S.W.R. in 1871 and at Chippenham and Stratton on the G.W.R. in 1873 and 1879 respectively. There was a consequent increase in dairy farming in north Wiltshire; the number of cattle there increased by 35 per cent between the 1870s and the 1910s, and the industry inverted the former economic disparity between the Chalk and Cheese Countries. For the first time in its history the latter, with its dairying, became more important than the sheep and corn country on the downlands. In addition access to railways and distant markets encouraged market-gardening on the poorer, sandy soils around Bromham, south of Calne.

This access to large but distant markets provided by the railways no doubt gave rise to some difficulties for the small local markets, and the effects have been disputed. Warminster, which had the largest corn-market in the west outside Bristol, was first served by railway in 1851 (although there was no through line till 1856) and went on growing for some years.

In 1854 the monthly *Warminster Miscellany* stated firmly that there was an 'increase [in local trade] due to the railway', but at the time of the 1871 census, when much of the downland was in economic decline, the registrar blamed a fall in Warminster's population since 1861 on 'railway communication', which he thought had 'diverted traffic' and led to 'inns closed, sack carriers etc. seek employment elsewhere'. At Wootton Bassett on the main line to Bristol, however, the registrar attributed growth to the 'general prosperity of trade' encouraged by the railway. It seems likely that in each case the railway assisted an economic trend rather than made it.

While the canals had little effect on the turnpiked roads, the railways had an immediate and disastrous effect on them. There was a temporary increase of traffic on such roads feeding railway stations, but a 75 per cent drop in traffic between most towns connected by railway. Every kind of agricultural as well as mineral and military traffic was taken by rail. In 1882 a flock of nearly two thousand sheep from the Scottish Borders arrived in two special trains at Trowbridge before being taken 16 miles south to repopulate the downland pastures at Kingston Deverill. Rabbits from these downs were sent to Smithfield, and Irish heifers came by train from Fishguard to refill Wiltshire valleys.

But even if the railways contributed to rural depopulation in the south, the establishment of the railway works at Swindon led to a compensating and rapid growth of that town. It had been a 'village' of 1,198 inhabitants in 1801. It was a small town of 4,879 in 1851. Before 1861 it had overtaken Trowbridge and about 1862 overtook Salisbury.

Swindon in 1828

Abbey Mills, Bradford on Avon

By 1901, with a population of 45,000, it was by far the largest town in the county.

Textiles

Other industries, while not stagnating, had shown nothing like the growth of the railways, and the Swindon workshops of the Great Western alone employed 13,000 people (more than the population of Salisbury) at their zenith. The cloth industry had been given a boost in the early 19th century by the opening of the Somerset Coal Canal. The cost of coal had severely inhibited the use of steam power in Wiltshire, but with the opening of the canal it was halved and within a month a steam factory had been opened at Trowbridge. New factory sites along the river Biss had been made available at Trowbridge after the sale of the site of its medieval castle, but the river could not supply much more of the power required and by 1821 about ninety per cent of the cloth industry's needs there were being supplied by new steam engines. Most of the engines were provided by the Birmingham makers Boulton and Watt, but some were made locally by Haden, a former apprentice of Boulton and Watt, and some by an inventive native, John Dyer. Trowbridge had now weathered the post-Napoleonic War depression and, with the building of 500 new houses, the population grew from 6,000 in 1811 to 9,500 in 1821, overtaking Salisbury and becoming temporarily the largest town in Wiltshire.

The county's textile industry embraced steam power on an extensive scale and faster than its rivals. By 1838, 64 per cent of the power in its factories was (or was capable of being) generated by steam. By 1850 it was 77 per cent while at Trowbridge it had risen to 90 per cent, but in most places the steam power was additional to existing sources of water power and steam was generated most often when extra demand or, more commonly, low water levels made it desirable. Nevertheless not all the clothiers turned so happily to steam, more particularly those who were further from coalfields. One at Warminster kept a horse-mill for his textile processing and used his steam-engine solely for shredding root-crops for his horses.

The returns of factory inspectors for 1838 showed the further concentration that had taken place in the cloth industry. Of 53 factories inspected, 19 were in Trowbridge, eight at Westbury, four each at Bradford on Avon and Calne, three at Bratton, two each at Chippenham and Melksham and one each at Christian Malford, Malmesbury, Holt and Heytesbury. Except for one silk factory at Calne these were cloth mills. There were also silk mills at Crockerton, Mere, Chippenham and Devizes. Little was left of the once flourishing textile industry of the Salisbury area, only two mills at Wilton and one at Harnham. The largest single employer was the mill at Crockerton, which was converted to silk spinning about 1805 by the Everett family, whose mill at Horningsham had been attacked in the mid-18th century.

106

Conditions in the mills were hard and large numbers of children were employed, particularly in silk spinning, working ten to twelve hours a day. Many of the owners made it clear to the factory inspectors that they thought they were performing a public service by employing children and making them work long hours, helping them to support their parents and keeping them out of mischief, while the factory inspectors had to admit in their reports that such children were at least as healthy as those outside. Even when restrictions were placed on the employment of children in factories they were not enforced as they should have been, as the inspectors recognised how dependent some of the poorer families were on the tiny earnings of their offspring. Unrest in the factory towns rarely ceased; though there was little recurrence of the violent riots of 1802 following which the 19-year-old Thomas Helliker was hung for criminal conspiracy, there were attacks on factories at Trowbridge in 1816 and 1817 when gigs – shearing machines – had been installed, and there were more widespread riots against the introduction of spring looms and about the reduction of wages in the 1820s. The latter protests were less common or violent than they were in the Frome valley in Somerset.

Population

At the beginning of the 19th century the county had a population of about one hundred and eighty-four thousand. Wiltshire then still included some outlying areas in Berkshire and Gloucestershire, which were transferred to those counties in 1844. The original census return for 1801 totalled 185,107 persons, but this was corrected later to 183,820. By the time of the more accurate census of 1851, after minor boundary changes, the total had risen to 254,000, and in 1901, after further changes (the parishes of Damerham and Martin were transferred to Hampshire, and Kilmington parish and part of Maiden Bradley were incorporated from Somerset), the total had risen to two hundred and seventy-one thousand. In Wiltshire, therefore, there was an increase of about forty per cent in the first half of the century. During the second half it was only seven per cent. For England and Wales as a whole the increases were 101 per cent and 81 per cent, and the difference between county and nation in the second half of the century is dramatic.

It had many causes. The most significant were the decline in farmwork on which the county was particularly dependent and the collapse of English corn prices nearer the end of the century. Next was a long depression in the county's main manufacturing industry, the cloth manufacture of west Wiltshire.

There had been net immigration to this area in the last half of the 18th century. This trend was reversed in the first half of the 19th century and emigration to other areas and abroad became massive during the last half. It has been suggested that population losses were more severe in the Chalk Country than the Cheese. This suggestion is true of the

SALISBURY
Penny Post

Salisbury postmark, 1826

107

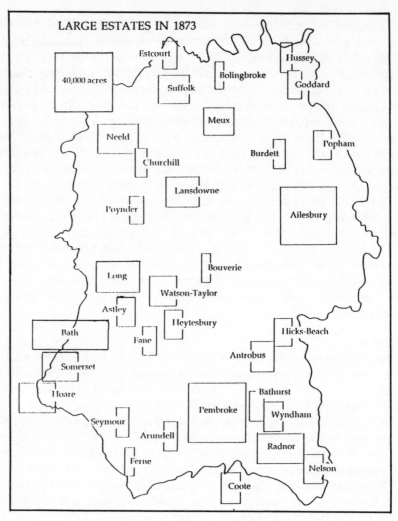

LARGE ESTATES IN 1873

Map 15.

most isolated downland areas but not so of the small towns and villages outside these special areas. If we exclude Swindon, population changes in Chalk and Cheese areas were closely parallel.

From 1801 to 1851 the growth in both Chalk and Cheese Countries outside the isolated downland parishes was about sixty per cent and the peak population of the century in most Wiltshire towns, villages and rural areas was reached between 1841 and 1861. From 1851 to 1871 there was little change in the population totals for either, but taking the whole second half of the 19th century there was a drop of about eight per cent in both Chalk and Cheese. The apparent difference between them is accounted for by the growth of Swindon in the last half of the century from five to forty-five thousand. Salisbury, which had been the largest town in the county at the beginning of the century and for some five centuries before that, grew by less than ten thousand in the century and was now well down the league table of English cities.

Arms of the Earl of Pembroke and Montgomery

Estates

Wiltshire had always been a county of large estates. Most grew larger at the expense of small farmers during the 19th century. Their peak may well have been reached about the time of the parliamentary inquiry into land-ownership which was set up in 1872. The figures for Wiltshire, based on the valuation lists for each parish in the county, were printed in 1875. They show that out of the 13,000 owners of land, 9,600 owned less than an acre and 4,400 owned more. There were 10 estates with more than 10,000 acres each, and they covered 23 per cent of the county (not 36 per cent as stated in Bateman's commentary on the report). Estates between 1,000 and 10,000 acres in extent occupied another 46 per cent of the county. Two hundred and nineteen owners obtained gross rentals of more than £1,000 per annum from lands in the county. The largest estates in order of size were:

Owner	Acres	Gross rental £ p.a.
Earl of Pembroke (Wilton)	39,600	43,200
Marquess of Ailesbury (Savernake)	38,000	40,000
Marquess of Bath (Longleat)	20,000	29,000
Earl Radnor (Longford)	17,200	21,500
S. Watson Taylor (Erlestoke)	15,000	21,000
Richard Long (Rood Ashton)	13,600	22,000
Sir John Neeld (Grittleton)	13,100	18,700
Sir Henry Meux's trustees (Vastern)	11,900	16,200
Marquess of Lansdowne (Bowood)	11,100	20,800
Earl of Suffolk (Charlton)	11,100	13,200

Of these landowners, Lord Bath owned another 8,000 acres in Somerset and even larger estates in Shropshire and Ireland, while Lord Lansdowne owned altogether 133,000 acres mainly in Scotland and Ireland. Lord Ashburton of the Grange, Hampshire, the Ecclesiastical Commissioners and Lord Normanton (another Hampshire resident) owned almost ten thousand acres each, while both the Duke of Somerset, of Maiden Bradley, and Sir Henry Hoare of Stourhead owned estates of about twelve thousand acres which straddled the border of Somerset and Wiltshire.

The inquiry did not reveal the extent of tenant holdings nor the rise of a dynasty of Strattons who, starting in the Vale of Pewsey, had made fortunes from early exploitation of the London milk market and were now spreading south to take on the prairies of the downland. Nor does it reveal the extent to which some estates, such as that of the Ailesburys, were burdened with debt and impoverished by their own extravagance.

Arms of the Marquess of Bath

109

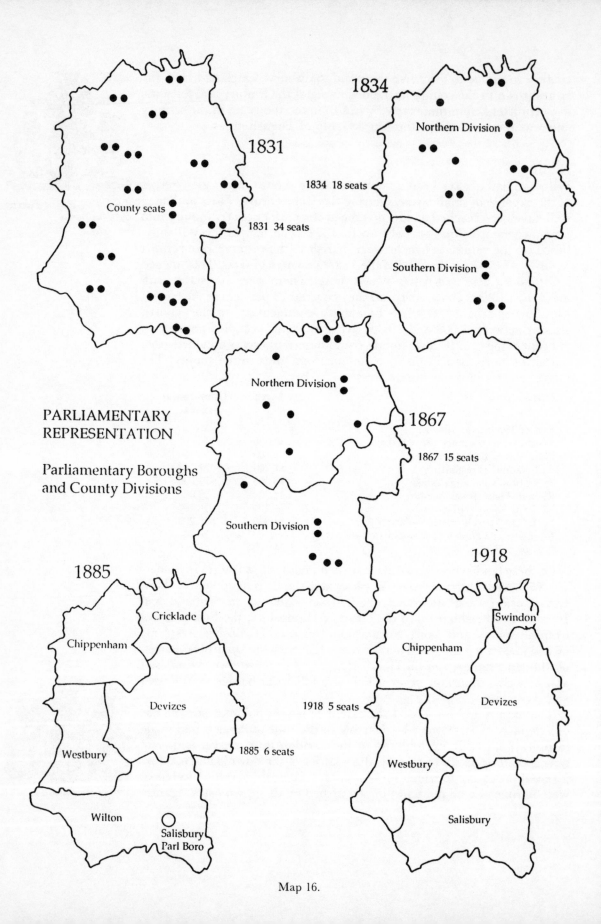

1831

1834

County seats

1831 34 seats

1834 18 seats

Northern Division

Southern Division

Northern Division

1867

1867 15 seats

Southern Division

PARLIAMENTARY
REPRESENTATION

Parliamentary Boroughs
and County Divisions

1885

Cricklade

Chippenham

Devizes

Westbury

Wilton

Salisbury
Parl Boro

1885 6 seats

1918

Swindon

Chippenham

Devizes

1918 5 seats

Westbury

Salisbury

Map 16.

Democracy?

By accidents rather than design, Wiltshire's representation in the parliament from feudal times down to the great Reform Act of 1832 was overweighted and eccentric. It started, as in other English counties, with two 'knights of the shire', who were elected by freeholders of the whole county, and two M.P.s for each borough. As there were 16 ancient boroughs in the county, it was represented by 34 members in all. Thus in the Reformation Parliament, which made Henry VIII undisputedly head of the English Church, Wiltshire had nearly twice as many M.P.s as its nearest rival and more than twice as many as Cornwall, Devon or Surrey. The neighbouring county of Gloucester had only four. The order was changed when kings created new boroughs, usually at a price for the benefit of the royal treasury. By 1563 Cornwall had taken first place from this cause alone, and in 1689, when Wiltshire still had 34 seats, Cornwall had 42, Yorkshire 28, Devon 26 and Hampshire twenty-four.

Arms of the Marquess of Lansdowne

None of this bore much relation to the size of county populations and the imbalance continued with little change right up to 1832. But Wiltshire was not only over-represented; the representation was also badly distributed. The borough of Old Salisbury (now called Old Sarum) had virtually ceased to exist and tiny boroughs like Bedwyn, Heytesbury and Hindon had little claim to separate representation when flourishing towns like Bradford, Trowbridge and Warminster lacked it. Over-representation got worse as the population of other areas of England grew. In 1801 Wiltshire's 34 Members represented a population of 184,000; Lancashire's 13 represented 673,000, i.e. one for 48 thousand people, while Middlesex had two for about half a million.

Perhaps worse, the representation of the boroughs became itself unrepresentative of them. Boroughs were expected to maintain their own M.P.s, and the small boroughs found it a considerable hardship. Thus within a short time most, and the city of Salisbury was generally an exception, were content to elect a gentleman who had little connection with the borough but was prepared to sit at his own expense and, with luck, might also pay his electors for the privilege. It was for this reason that various noble and important families were able to dominate the parliamentary representation of many boroughs for decades. Old Sarum continued to return two members from its empty borough, and the village borough of Heytesbury, which only included about half the settlement, was noteworthy for having no contested election for over 130 years: from 1689 down to its abolition in 1832.

County representation followed the same patterns. From the Reformation to the time of Charles I county representation was dominated by Seymours, Herberts, Hungerfords and Bayntons, then from Charles II to George II by the How and Hyde families, and from 1722 to 1812 by Goddards and Longs. There was more diffusion of power in the 18th

111

century, however, when newer names such as Astley of Everleigh (but formerly of Staffordshire), Benett of Pythouse and Methuen of Corsham came to command borough representation.

By the 1832 act seven of the Wiltshire boroughs lost their seats altogether, while the overall representation of the county was reduced to eighteen. The abolition of what Cobbett called 'these vile rotten holes' was so long overdue that it was not unwelcome even to John Benett of Pythouse, who was one of the most reactionary and hated men in the county because of his savage attitude to the poor. Wiltshire's representation was reduced by later acts to 15 seats in 1867, to six in 1885 and five in 1918.

Monuments

Monuments to this era of change are everywhere in the county though many are not appreciated as much as they deserve, perhaps because they are so numerous. The greatest are those of the railways which produced the most widespread and dramatic change in the history of the county. Particularly notable is the London-Bristol railway, whose line through Wiltshire includes the heaviest engineering works on its route: deep cuttings and the tunnel at Box, which was the longest in the country when it was made. Associated with the railway is the 'railway village' at Swindon of 243 houses designed by Matthew Digby Wyatt.

Another industrial housing estate of note is Prospect Square at Westbury. It was built in 1870 by Abraham Laverton, the Liberal cloth-manufacturer, to rehouse his work-people who had been evicted by his successful Tory rival after an election. Most other 19th-century housing is undistinguished, but a few country houses are worth mention: John Benett's new Pythouse, of 1805, and its imitation at Philipps House, Dinton, of 1816, which are both in a 'Grecian' style, and Tottenham House, rebuilt by Cundy in 1825 for the Ailesburys. Finally at the end of the century there is Philip Webb's 'Clouds', built for one of the Wyndhams at East Knoyle but now sadly mutilated.

There was considerable building and alteration of churches. Between 1837 and 1887, 45 completely new churches were built. These included Wyatt and Brandon's grand, Italianate, new church for the Herberts at Wilton, and Pearson's churches at Sutton Veny and Chute Forest. In addition 32 others were enlarged in the same period and 98 restored, most by the advisory architect to the diocese, T. H. Wyatt.

Other monuments are the town halls, symbols of rising civic pride, at Devizes, Melksham, Westbury and Warminster, nearly all of the early 19th century; the larger mills, particularly Laverton's Angel Mill at Westbury, Greenland Upper Mill at Bradford and the mill at Quemerford; and last but not least the bank premises in almost every town in the county. These latter represent the rising wealth of the country as a whole, of which Wiltshire did not receive a proportionate share.

Cottage, Swindon railway village

112

45. A turnpike tollhouse on Boreham Road, Warminster. This was on the Salisbury road made under the 18th-century turnpike acts by the Warminster Trust.

46. Caen Hill locks on the Kennet & Avon Canal at Devizes. This flight of locks, the second longest in England, was completed in 1810.

47. The Engine House, Swindon, a drawing by J. C. Bourne in *History and Description of the Great Western Railway* (1846).

48. Abbey Mills, Bradford on Avon. Built as a cloth factory in 1857, it was converted to a rubber factory and is now used as offices.

49. Prospect Square, Westbury. Model industrial housing of 1870, built by Abraham Laverton, a Liberal cloth manufacturer, to house his work-people who had been evicted after an election by his successful Tory rival.

50. Marlborough Town Hall, erected 1902, and the tower of St Mary's church. The main Saxon settlement was around St Mary's, at the east end of the present town. The Norman castle was at the west end, in the grounds of Marlborough College.

51. Avon Mill, Malmesbury. Once a cloth mill, it was converted to a silk works in the 19th century, and later into an antique furniture warehouse.

52. Windmill Hill Business Park, Swindon: British Aerospace offices reflecting the windmill, brought from Chiseldon.

XI Modern Wiltshire

The 19th century ended and the 20th century began symbolically for Wiltshire with a gale which blew down one of the great stones of Stonehenge. Its two great industries, farming and cloth manufacture, were in decline and it is surprising that the county's population was not lower than the 271,000 which it had struggled to reach by 1901.

In the first 30 years of the new century its population grew by 11 per cent, but this was still 'stagnant' by comparison with most of England, while the loss of population from the rural areas was considerable. Villages like Alderton and Foxley in the Cheese Country of north Wiltshire and Compton Chamberlayne and Imber in the Chalk south, lost nearly half their populations during that period. Seemingly big gains were made by Chippenham, which grew by 60 per cent, and Salisbury, which increased by 48 per cent, but in real numbers only the addition of 5,500 people to Swindon, which grew by 39 per cent, was large. Their growth reflected the continued prosperity of the railway and other engineering works at Swindon and Chippenham, and of the market function of the cathedral city.

The Great Bustard, once a common bird on Salisbury Plain. The last native was killed near Warminster in 1830. Attempts have been made to reintroduce breeding pairs (imported from Hungary) at Porton Down

The armed services

In the rural areas the only notable growth was on the eastern side of Salisbury Plain, around Durrington and Tidworth where the Army had now gained a considerable foothold. The Army had used the northern Plain for much of the late 19th century and had obtained training rights over some eight hundred square miles in 1872, in part to establish safer artillery ranges, for cannon-fire had been practised on Woolwich Common until a cadet was hit by a cannon-ball, and in part and more importantly for cavalry training exercises. It was certainly good galloping country though poor for other sports once the last of the Great Bustards which once roamed the Plain vanished in the early 19th century. The Army went on to purchase some forty thousand acres of this land in 1897, two-thirds to the west and one-third to the east of the Avon. They bought the downland involved for about £10 an acre, the going price at that time, though the price fell lower in the 20th century and only rose sharply after the Second World War. To improve communication between the two training areas they also bought some of the valley farms in the Durrington and Figheldean area, though at a much higher price. Some of the valley farmers resented approaches by the Army but the landowners of the impoverished downland were content

113

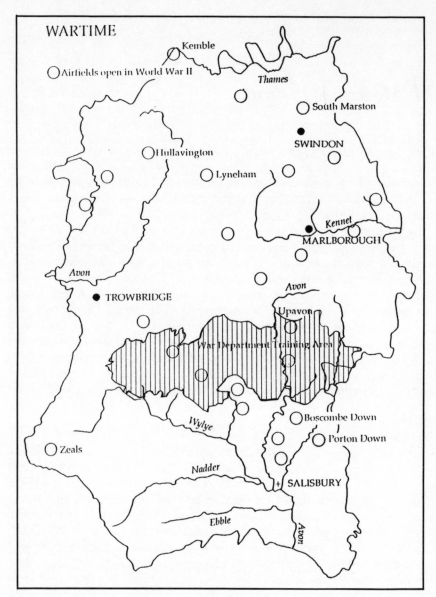

WARTIME

Kemble

○ Airfields open in World War II

Thames

○ South Marston

● SWINDON

○ Hullavington

Lyneham

Kennet

● MARLBOROUGH

Avon

● TROWBRIDGE

Avon

Upavon

War Department Training Area

Wylye

Boscombe Down

Porton Down

○ Zeals

Nadder

+ SALISBURY

Ebble

Avon

Map 17.

enough to sell, and the general feeling was probably summed up by Sir Henry Malet, one of the owners, when he said 'I rejoice to think that Salisbury Plain is likely to realise its manifest destiny as the training ground of the British Army'.

114

Permanent camps were established at Tidworth and Bulford, the 'London' end of the area, in 1902 and a permanent base was built for the School of Artillery at Larkhill, west of the Avon, in 1914. It was the steady enlargement of these establishments which accounted for the considerable growth of population in this formerly-isolated area, which Pepys had needed guides to reach from Salisbury. Most of the Plain was occupied by the Army during the First World War, and temporary camps were made and often connected to temporary railway lines round the fringes of its extended training areas.

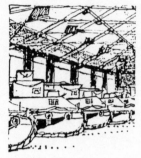

Tanks at Warminster

The total contribution of Wiltshire to the 1914 War cannot be measured. War memorials in every town and village show the sacrifice in lives. Of the Wiltshire Regiment, which served in many theatres of war, five thousand died.

Following this war, activity in and around Salisbury Plain actually increased. Ordnance workshops were set up at Tidworth in the early 1920s and were greatly expanded in 1938 and 1939. Further workshops for the repair of all War Department vehicles were established at Warminster at the western end of the training area in 1938, more purchases of land having been made by the Department, increasing their holding on the Plain to some ninety-two thousand acres.

In the preparations for the invasion of Europe, in the later stages of the Second World War, extensive road improvements south of the Plain were made towards the south coast and, in addition, the vehicle bases were lent to the U.S. Army. Both were returned to Southern Command in 1945 and Warminster became the Command's main workshop.

The air force too had its share of the Plain and spread over other areas during the Second World War. The first military airfield here, and the first in the country, was opened at Larkhill in 1909, and another, now the oldest active airfield in Britain, was opened at Upavon in 1912. The field at Boscombe Down near Amesbury, whose 'Weighbridge Hangar' is a dominant feature of the eastern approaches to the Plain, has played an important part in the testing and development of military aircraft. Another near Stonehenge posed a threat to that ancient monument when it was claimed that the stones were a hazard to aircraft. Many others which were more or less temporary were opened in the Second World War. Most of these were, like Boscombe Down, on old downland, but some like Castle Combe and Cricklade (and a large part of the Kemble field) were in the extreme north. North of the Marlborough Downs the field at Lyneham opened in 1942 was important as a transport centre (and played an important part in the Falklands War) while in the extreme south-west a less useful field near Zeals was opened where several aircraft came to a sticky end in its heavy clay subsoil.

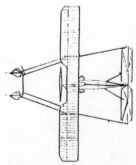

Cody's 'Cathedral', winner of the military aircraft trials on the Plain in 1912

The great estates

The increased taxes on inherited property, usually known as 'Death Duties', had a growing effect on this county of large estates as the century

Arms of the Marquess of Ailesbury

progressed. They were first introduced by a Conservative administration in 1889, but were notably increased by following Liberal governments and particularly by Lloyd George in 1909, and they hit the large landowners heavily after each World War when so many of the young heirs were killed. They were influential in the break-up of the Antrobus estate, centred on Amesbury Abbey, in 1915, the sale of much outlying farmland on the Pembroke's Wilton estate in 1917 and 1918, the vast reduction of the Thynnes' Longleat estate in 1919 and again in 1947, and the sale of the Savernake estate round the Ailesburys' Tottenham House in 1929. In addition taxes contributed to the St Johns leaving Lydiard Tregoze where they had been for some centuries, the Pophams selling Littlecote which they had acquired in the early 17th century, and the Longs leaving their huge mansion at Rood Ashton to sad decay. This of course had a knock-on effect on the farming of the county and greatly extended the number of owner-occupiers and the land they held, which was less than 10 per cent of the county in 1914 but had risen to 37 per cent in 1941 and nearly 85 per cent by 1983.

Farming

More widespread owner-occupation did not bring any greater prosperity to the county's farming. The total acreage under cultivation declined slowly but continuously and the number of sheep, which had once been the mainstay of Wiltshire farming, declined by a third between 1870 and 1914 and was halved again by 1924. There was, however, an increase in milk-production which was in part due to the introduction of the movable milking parlour, invented by the Wiltshire engineer A. J. Hosier of Wexcombe, and some have said that 'Friesians replaced sheep'. Cultivated land declined about five per cent in the first decade of the century and by another 10 per cent by the 1930s. Arable was halved in this long period of decline and fallow increased by a third. Sheep fell to their lowest total ever, 162,000, by 1939.

Wiltshire has not been renowned in the popular modern sport of identifying deserted villages. Some certainly faded to little in the Middle Ages and many, like Hill and Kingston Deverills, shifted their centres and lost some population without disappearing. The 20th century, however, produced two clearly deserted villages. The first was at Snap near Aldbourne, the second at Imber near Warminster, both in the Chalk Country.

The former small village of Snap and its surrounding fields were bought by a butcher from Ramsbury who converted them to raise cattle and slowly closed the houses of the village as their tenants died or migrated. While there is a local tradition that the village was lost because the water supply failed, this is not the case. The last tenant moved (probably breathing a sigh of relief) to Aldbourne and the now-redundant church and school were sold off about 1905. Only earthworks now remain.

Imber church

116

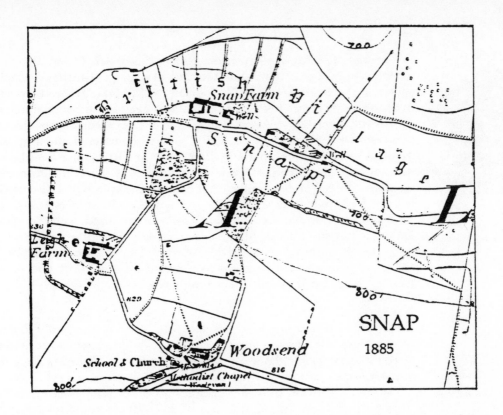

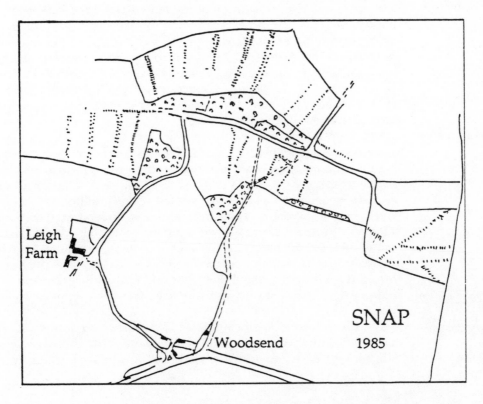

Fig. 8. **A TWENTIETH CENTURY DESERTED VILLAGE**
Snap, near Aldbourne, in 1885 and 1985

'City of Truro', built at Swindon in 1903, the first locomotive to reach 100 miles an hour

The loss of 'Little Imber on the Down, Seven miles from any town' is better known. It had a population of 500 at its peak in 1841, which is surprising for so isolated a place. This fell to 152 by 1931 and the village might perhaps have vanished from natural causes if it had not been in the middle of the large Army training area. Its inhabitants were virtually prisoners for times in the First World War when practice shelling badly damaged local houses. In 1939, after the War Department had bought most of the village, the area was again subject to dangerous bombardment and, in November 1943 with the imminent arrival of United States forces, the inhabitants were given six weeks to leave. Their hopes of returning later, which they felt they had been promised, were frustrated, for the area was retained after the war by the Ministry of Defence for active battle training. Soon only the medieval stone church remained of the village's former buildings, most of the rest, being of cob and thatch, having crumbled from shell-shock and neglect.

New industries

Employment in farming went on declining and provided only four per cent of Wiltshire's total employment by 1981. The same was true of the cloth industry during the century. The last weavers closed in 1982. But new industries had risen from the old.

The trade in fresh milk to London and other big towns which had been made possible by the railways in the 19th century, now led to the development of the preparation of condensed and dried milk, sometimes in old cloth mills like those used by the *Nestlé* company at Chippenham and Staverton. This new trade helped to even out the supply and demand problems of the industry, and to mop up an increasing surplus of liquid milk. Unfortunately the older-established cheese industry, which included most of the 'Double Gloucester', actually largely produced in north Wiltshire, has been wiped out by the spread of the universal and often misnamed 'Cheddar'.

An important bacon and meat-pie industry grew up at Calne and then spread to Chippenham and Trowbridge. In this the most successful firm was that of Harris of Calne, who had brought the railway there in 1863. Their factory had employed 2,000 in 1957 and was a landmark on the old Bath Road. The business had started with the killing of surplus pigs which were being driven from Ireland to the London market along the old road; Wiltshire farmers never supplied more than about fifteen per cent of its needs for bacon pigs when the industry was most flourishing. It declined in the 1970s, and the business at Calne was closed and the factory demolished in the 1980s. The industry still survives at Trowbridge where it has spread into the area formerly occupied by textile mills.

The silk industry, mostly spinning, which had been introduced in the early 19th century in many parts of the county, from Marlborough and Salisbury to Mere, to provide work for unemployed textile workers,

A Scout charabanc

118

could not stand competition from French imports once protective import tariffs were removed, and collapsed by the early 20th century, but many of the works were re-used for other small manufactures. The great cloth mill at Malmesbury, which was converted into the last big silk works, became an antique furniture showroom, but that at Crockerton was demolished. Its offshoot at Warminster was converted to engineering and other enterprises.

Swindon railway works

The railway industry, which was still maturing at the beginning of the century, spawned new demands which were met by the new small enterprises. Brake and signal works were successfully introduced down-line from Swindon at Chippenham (where some of the first locomotives for the London-Bristol railway had been made but found wanting), and the manufacture of rubber for railway and other vehicle springs was introduced into old mills at Bradford, Limpley Stoke and Melksham. From this rubber business arose the first production of rubber tyres for motor cars at Melksham in 1906. The engine of much of this scattered development, the giant railway workshops at Swindon, continued to expand right up to the great depression between the two World Wars and, indeed, its employment helped Wiltshire to weather this bad period better than neighbouring counties. By 1939 the railway works had spread over 326 acres, of which 79 were covered, and even then, at its downturn to a long decline, it employed some eleven thousand people. During the two World Wars the shops were converted largely to the making of munitions, but by 1950, when they were restored to their original purpose, they were servicing 4,000 locomotives, 8,000 carriages and 86,000 wagons. The works provided predominantly male employment, but good use was made in the mid-century of the tradition of engineering skill as well as the pool of underemployed females by introducing many other skilled jobs to Swindon. Before and during the Second World War many companies were evacuated here from London and vulnerable coastal towns, and stayed afterwards. After the war more were attracted and helped to fill the gap caused by the slow collapse and closure of the railway workshops, which ended their long life here in 1987.

Many of the minor engineering industries naturally had a close connection with farming and other local trades, like the agricultural engineers Brown & May of Devizes, Reeves of Bratton and J. Wallis Titt of Warminster, and the millwrights and heating engineers such as the Hadens, who concentrated at Trowbridge. But many of their products, like the wind-pumps of Wallis Titt, were sold throughout the world.

In spite of its early connection with rubber tyres, however, and its pre-occupations in two world wars with vehicles of all kinds from bicycles to tanks and aircraft, Wiltshire took no lead in the development of the motor car itself, though the small company of Scout at Salisbury made a few motor cars early in the century and then motor-coaches.

An early steam engine made by Brown and May of Devizes

119

With the general introduction of the car, however, there started a long drift of population back to the countryside. This took some time, for in the meantime the continued improvement of urban services such as gas, electricity, piped water and main drainage emphasised the towns' superior environment and led to further losses of rural population.

It was only in the 1930s that the spread of motor cars, still a middle-class luxury, and the conversion of the former potholed and dusty roads to smooth clean highways, made the countryside a particularly desirable place to live (while, generally, earning daily bread in a nearby town). Unlike the railways, which had fostered dense settlements round railway stations, the rise of the motor car led to ribbons of bungalows along all the main roads of the county and ugly new villages on former army camps in still-beautiful downland around Salisbury. The inter-war scars of such development are only now being healed by the growth of garden trees and shrubs.

Farming and landscape changes

Immense capital investment was made in farming during World War Two, particularly to restore the fertility and increase production on the run-down Chalk Country where in many places rabbits were as valuable a harvest as crops. But with the addition of still more farm machinery, labour on the land steadily declined. Apart from loss of employment the chief post-World War Two changes have been the increase of arable land to its 1900 level and the increase of barley cultivation to more than four times its pre-war levels. The policy of 'taking the plough round the farm' has been extended so that between 1961 and 1985 the amount of 'permanent grass' was further reduced from some 39 per cent of the farmland to 29 per cent. The number of cattle remained fairly steady but the number of sheep doubled and the number of poultry greatly increased.

Because of all this very little of the old downland turf and its interesting flora was left, and the Nature Conservancy Council had to buy a farm at Winterbourne Stoke to preserve some of the last remaining. The average visitor did not greatly feel the significant changes in the Chalk Country, however, as he usually visualised both 'Plain' and 'Downs' as great unhedged prairies. To him, the changes in north Wiltshire might have seemed more startling because of the more notice-able and steady removal of hedges and the huge loss of elms, the favourite hedgerow tree of the area, due to Dutch elm disease. The county and district councils have, however, recognised the aesthetic and economic value of their landscapes and have devoted much time and money to tree planting and other restoration.

The M4

Three extensive 'areas of outstanding natural beauty' have been designated by the Countryside Commission (for the Cotswold fringe, the Marlborough Downs and for West Wiltshire Downs and Cranborne Chase) and 165 'Conservation Areas' have been created by county and

120

district councils in attempts to preserve their existing beauty and interest. These vary from the county's best-known village, Castle Combe, to the railway works at Swindon designated on their closure in 1987.

Arms of the Borough of Swindon, granted in 1903

Population

Most of the county's war-time 'refugee' industries have stayed and flourished, while the country villages, particularly along the chalk streams, have attracted the retirement of wealthier immigrants from the south-east. By 1981 the population had grown to 518,545, an increase of 17 per cent above the 303,000 of 1931. Of this one fifth lived in Swindon, which had reached 104,000 and was still growing fast. The growth of this town was distorting the county's balance of industry and population, particularly after its expansion under a town development scheme agreed in 1952 with the former London County Council to take some 'excess' population from London. It was also greatly assisted by its success in bending the London to South Wales motorway, which had been planned to pass through the Kennet valley, to run instead over the Marlborough Downs and to give rapid access to both sides of the town.

Swindon is still three times larger than the next biggest Wiltshire town, Salisbury, which has woken from its somewhat somnolent pre-war state to meet its potential as a market and business centre for the widest of such catchment areas in the county. In this it has attempted to rebuild its central area and, like Coventry, to pile its car-parks on top of its shopping development. Criticism of some of its cruder developments left it with a prominent central road and bridge leading nowhere, which were later removed at further expense. After Salisbury, the largest towns in 1981 were Trowbridge with 23,000, Chippenham with 19,000 and Warminster with fifteen thousand. Immigration accounts for much of these totals. Between 1961 and 1971 it reached 45 per cent in the Rural District adjoining Swindon, 27 per cent at Calne and 24 per cent at Warminster, where it was also assisted by the London County Council. But in spite of this immigration, which slowed down in following years, Wiltshire is still a very rural county with a population density of only 1.5 persons per hectare (every person having nearly two acres). Of the present English counties it is now thirty-ninth in total population and, from being one of the most populated areas of the country in the centuries before the Romans came, it is now one of the least, tenth from bottom of the English league.

Arms of Wiltshire County Council, granted 1937

Local government reorganisation

By 1974 it had been generally recognised that low and scattered populations in small units were difficult and expensive to administer, and there was a nation-wide re-organisation of local government. The county as a whole was not mutilated as happened to all its neighbours, but its

121

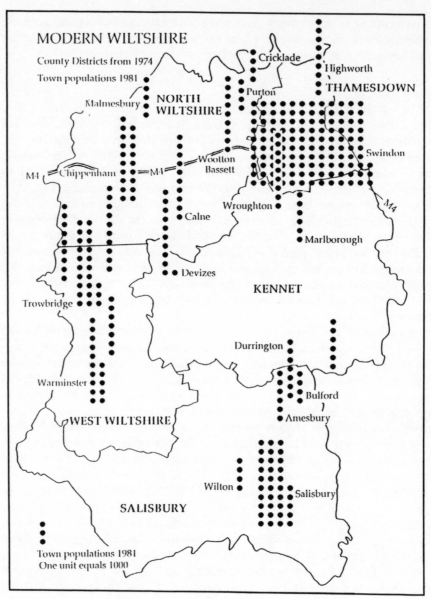

Map 18.

25 former local authorities, which varied in size and population from the 2,500 of Malmesbury to the (then) 91,000 of Swindon, were amalgamated into five new districts, which were named North Wiltshire, Thamesdown (largely Swindon), West Wiltshire, Kennet and Salisbury. Few have

much in common with their district centres and it is doubtful if the changes have shown the economy and increased efficiency which was promised.

Trends
Wiltshire today is similar to its neighbours in its present age-structure and its population trends. In comparison with the whole of England, its birthrate is slightly higher and its death rate lower. It has a low rate of illegitimacy and a high ratio of cars to people (375 per 1,000 compared with 314 in England as a whole). Its gross domestic product per head in 1981 and its employment and earnings in 1987 were all above those of the neighbouring counties. The differences are not great, but its future does look brighter now than it has done for at least two centuries.

Swindon railway station, 1845, showing 'broad-gauge' rails and carriages

For Further Study

County Bibliographies
Chandler, J., *Studying Wiltshire: Information for Local Historians* (1982); Goddard, E. H., *Wiltshire Bibliography* (1929); Green, R. A. M., *A Bibliography of Printed Works . . . Wiltshire 1920-1960* (1975).

General History
Bettey, J. H., *Wessex from AD 1000* (1986); Burnett, David, *A Wiltshire Portrait, 1568-1856* [drawings, etc.] (1983); Burnett, David, *A Wiltshire Camera, 1835-1914* (1975); Burnett, David, *A Wiltshire Camera, 1914-45* (1976); Cunliffe, B., *Wiltshire to AD 1000* (forthcoming); Hoare, R. Colt, *The Ancient History of Wiltshire*, 2 vols. (new edn. 1975); Hoare, R. Colt, *The History of Modern Wiltshire*, 6 vols. (1822-43); Marshman, M., *A Wiltshire Landscape: Scenes from the Countryside, 1920-40* (1984); *Victoria History of the County of Wiltshire*, 14 vols. (1953-continuing); Wiltshire Record Society volumes (usually annually).

Periodicals
Hatcher Review (biannually); *Journal of the Wiltshire Family History Society* (biannually); *Wiltshire Archaeological Magazine* (annually).

Geology
Barron, R. S., *The Geology of Wiltshire* (1976).

Archaeology
Burl, A., *Prehistoric Avebury* (1979); Chippindale, C., *Stonehenge Complete* (1983); Osborne, G., *Exploring Ancient Wiltshire* (1982); Richards, J., *Beyond Stonehenge* (1985); *Victoria History of the County of Wiltshire*, Vol. 1.

Architecture
Pevsner, N., and Cherry, B., *Buildings of England: Wiltshire* (2nd edn. 1973); Royal Commission on Historical Monuments, *Inventory of the Historical Monuments in the City of Salisbury*, Vol. 1 (1980); Royal Commission on Historical Monuments, *Churches of South-east Wiltshire* (1987).

Domesday
Darby, H. C., *Domesday Geography of South-west England* (1977); Thorn, C. and F. (eds.), *Domesday Book: Wiltshire* (1979) [text and translation]; *Victoria History of the County of Wiltshire*, Vol. 2.

Industry
Corfield, M. C., *A Guide to the Industrial Archaeology of Wiltshire* (1978); Rogers, K. H., *Warp and Weft* (1986); *Victoria History of the County of Wiltshire*, Vol. 4.

Land Use
Davis, Thomas, *General View of the Agriculture of Wiltshire* (1811); Fry, A. H., *Land Utilization: Wiltshire* (1940).

Placenames
E. Ekwall, *The Concise Oxford Dictionary of English Place Names* (4th edn. 1980); Gover, J. E. B., *The Place Names of Wiltshire* (1939).

Population
Census Returns from 1801-1981; *Victoria History of the County of Wiltshire*, Vol. 4.

Other major sources of information on Wiltshire are: the Local Studies Libraries of the County Council at Library H.Q., Trowbridge, Sheep Street, Devizes, Salisbury Market Place, and Swindon Reference Library; the Wiltshire Record Office at Trowbridge; and the Museums at Devizes (Long Street) and Salisbury (King's House).

124

Index

A Court, Charles, Asst. Poor Law
    Commissioner, 96, 98
Adam's Grave, battles at, 30, 33
Adlam, John, of Westbury, 66
Aethelred II ('the Unready'), 36
Ailesbury, Earl of (Brudenell-
    Bruce), 82, 92, 98, 109
Aldbourne, 55, 57
Alderton, 113
Aldhelm, Bishop and Saint, 33,
    35, 37
Alfred, King of Wessex ('the
    Great'), 30, 33, 35, 36
Alvediston, 39
Ambrosius, 28
Amesbury Abbey (& estate), 57,
    65, 66, 80, 95, 100, 116
Andover Union (workhouse), 97,
    98
Arthur, leader of Britons, 30, 31
Arundell family, of Wardour, 70,
    74, 78, 89
Ashton Keynes, 41
Astley family, of Everleigh, 112
Athelstan, 36
Atrebates, 23
Aubrey, John, 9, 16
Avebury, 10, 16, 17
Avon, River: Bristol, 18, 54, 58,
    101; Salisbury, 9, 18, 21, 26,
    42, 50, 93, 101
Ayscough (Bishop of Salisbury),
    59

Badon, battle of, 30
Barbury Castle, 30
Barford, 23
Barrington, Shute (Bishop of
    Salisbury), 83
Bath, 24, 31, 36, 58, 87, 88, 99,
    109
Bath, Marquess of, see Thynne
Battlesbury, 21
Bayeux, Bishop of, 40
Baynton: family, 111; Sir Edward,
    69, 76
Bec, Abbey of, 41, 47, 63

Becket, Thomas à, 46
Beckford family, 90
Bede, 28
Bedwyn, 35, 39, 43, 45, 53, 101,
    103, 111
Bemerton, 74
Benett: Thomas, 77; John, 95, 112
Berwick St Leonard, 80
Biddestone, 58
Birinus (Bishop of Dorchester), 31
Black Death, 54, 56
Blackwell (or Backwell) Hall,
    54, 62, 87
Bokerley Dyke, 26
Bolingbroke (St John) family, 88
Boscombe Down, 23
Bouverie family, 82
Bowl's Barrow (nr. Heytesbury),
    18
Bowood, 89, 90, 104, 109
Box, 88, 101, 104, 112
Boyton, 87
Bradenstoke, 65
Bradford on Avon, 35, 36, 44, 58,
    73, 87, 88, 96, 98, 100, 106,
    111, 112, 119
Bradley, North, 87
Bratton, 35, 106, 119
Bray (Berks.), Vicar of, 68
Braydon Forest, 43, 73
Bremhill, 57, 87
Bristol, 53, 54, 58, 62, 76, 77,
    100, 101, 103, 104, 105, 119
Britford, 37
Brixton Deverill, 47, 63
Bromham, 69, 105
Brown, Lancelot, 90
Brown & May, of Devizes, 119
Bruce and Brudenell-Bruce
    family, 89; see also Tottenham
Bruges, Ludlow, 96
Brunel, Isambard Kingdom, 104
Bulford, 115
Bulkington, 68
Burnett, Gilbert (Bishop of
    Salisbury), 83
Bury Wood, Colerne, 21
Bush Barrow, 19
Button, Sir William, 77
By Brook, 54, 58

Cade, Jack, rebellion of, 1450, 58
Calne, 35, 36, 39, 43, 83, 96, 104,
    106, 118, 121
Campeggio, Cardinal, Bishop of
    Salisbury, 63, 68
Capon, Bishop of Salisbury, 67,
    68
Castle Combe, 55, 58, 115
Castle Eaton, 68
Catuvellauni, 23, 24
Caus, Isaac de, 80
Ceawlin, 31
Cerdic, 31
Charford (Hants), battle at, 31
Charles: I, 74, 77, 111; II, 77, 78,
    111
Charlton, nr. Downton, 57
Charlton Park, 89, 91, 109
Cherhill, 13
Chichester, 24
Chicklade, 86
Chilmark, 9, 46
Chippenham, 35, 43, 45, 57, 87,
    100, 104, 105, 106, 113, 118,
    119, 121
Chisbury, 35
Chisenbury, 26
Chitterne, 99
Christian Malford, 106
Churchill, John (later Duke of
    Marlborough), 80
Chute Forest, 43, 45, 112
Cirencester (Glos.), alias Corinium,
    24, 31, 58, 99
Clack Castle, 41
Clarendon: Earls of, see Hyde;
    Forest and Palace, 43, 45-6,
    49
Claudius, Emperor of Rome, 23,
    24
Cleyhill, 69
Cnut, King of Denmark and
    England, 36
Cobbett, William, 93, 96, 100
Cockayne, Alderman of London,
    73
Codford St Peter, 37
Cogidubnus, 24
Cold Kitchen Hill, 26
Colerne, 37, 55

Collingbourne, 45
Commius, 23
Compton Chamberlayne, 77, 113
Coneybury Hill, 16
Constantine: I, Emperor of Rome, 26; II, Emperor of Rome, 28
Corsham, 57, 84, 87, 101
Corsham Court, 70, 89, 90
Corsley, 86
Cottington, Baron, 77
Coutances, Bishop of, 40
Cranbourne Chase, 14; 26, 120
Cranmer, Archbishop, 73
Cricklade, 34, 35, 36, 44, 46, 53, 101, 115
Crockerton, 84, 87, 106, 119
Croke family, 45
Cromwell: Oliver (Lord Protector), 76, 77; Thomas, 60, 63
Cunetio, (nr. Mildenhall), 26, 28
Cynegils, 32
Cynric, 31

Damerham (now in Hants), 57, 107
Danby, Earl of, 77
Danvers, Sir John: 1588, 69; Regicide, 77
Darell (or Darrell) family, of Littlecote, 69, 70
Daubeny, General, 60
Dauntsey, 69
Dauntsey's School (Lavington), 83
Davenant, John (Bishop of Salisbury), 74
Davis, Thomas, 86, 92, 96
Defoe, Daniel, 99
Devizes, 9, 46, 48, 57, 58, 59, 62, 71, 76, 77, 82, 98, 100, 101, 102, 106, 112, 115
Dinton, Phillips House, 112
Donheads, 57
Dorchester: Dorset, 24; Oxon., 31
Downton, 13, 39, 41, 45, 46, 50, 53, 54, 98
Duke, George, of Lake House, 70
Durnford, 96
Durocornovium (Wanborough), 26
Durotriges, 23
Durrington, 54, 113
Durrington Walls, 16, 17
Dyer, John, 106
Dyrham (Glos.), battle at, 31

Eadgar, King of Wessex and England, 36
Easton Down, 12
Easton Royal, 65, 66, 70

Ebsbury, 23
Ecbrytesstan, 35
Edington Priory, 35, 59, 63, 66, 67
Edmund Ironside, 36
Edward: the Confessor, 36, 39; I, 49; III, 46, 53; VI, 61, 67, 73; Earl of Salisbury, 47
Ela, Countess of Salisbury, 47, 51
Elcot, 53
Elias of Dereham, 52
Elizabeth I, 68, 71, 73
Enton, 41
Eppillus, 23
Erlestoke, 90, 105
Esturmy (or Sturmy) family, 45
Everett family, 88
Everleigh, 55, 95
Exeter (Devon), 24, 31, 33, 60, 77, 100

Fairfax, General, 76
Fargo plantation (Stonehenge), 16
Farleigh Hungerford (Somerset), 57
Fastolf, Sir John, 58
Fiennes, Celia, 99
Figheldean, 113
Fonthill, 49, 80, 90
Fowlswick (nr. Malmesbury), 49
Foxley, 113
Frome Valley (Somerset), 62, 107

George: II, 111; III, 82
Gildas, 30
Glastonbury Abbey estates, 33, 39, 40, 41, 47, 49, 54, 57
Gloucester, 31, 33
Goddard family, 68, 70, 82, 111
Golden Barrow (Upton Lovell), 19
Gorges, Sir Thomas, of Longford, 70, 82
Gough Map, 100
Great Chalfield, 59
Great Cheverell, 83
Great Ridge, 26, 42
Gresham, Sir Thomas, 69
Grittleton (Neeld estate), 109
Guthrum, 33

Hadens, 106, 119
Ham, 41
Hamshill Ditches, 26
Hanging Longford, 23
Hannington, 57, 86
Hardenhuish church, 84
Harnham (Salisbury), 52, 53
Harold: Earl of Wessex, 36, 38, 39; Hardrada, 36

Harris, bacon curers, of Calne, 104, 118
Hastings: battle of, 36; family, 60
Helliker, Thomas, 107
Hengist and Horsa, 30
Hengistbury Head, 21
Henry: I, 46; II, 45, 46, 47; III, 45, 51, 53; V, 58; VII, 60; VIII, 60, 63
Herbert: Earls of Pembroke and Montgomery, 61, 66, 111; George, 74; Sidney, 98
Herman, Bishop of Sherbourne, Ramsbury & Salisbury, 44
Hertford, Lord, see Seymour
Heytesbury, 50, 57, 67, 86, 106, 111
Highworth, 38, 50, 86, 97, 100
Hill Deverill, 69, 72, 116
Hindon, 50, 95, 111
Hinton Charterhouse, 63
Hoare family, of Stourhead, 90, 109
Hod Hill (Dorset), 24
Holt, 88, 106
Honorius: Roman General, 28; III, Pope, 56
Hopton, Sir Ralph, 76
Horningsham, 84, 87
Horton: Thomas, 59, 62; Edward, 69
Hosier, A. J., milking parlour of, 116
How (or Howe) family, 82, 111
Hungerford: (Berks.), 100; family, 57, 60, 69, 76, 111
Hunt, John, of Enford, 69
Hyde: Anne, Queen to James II, 78; Edward, Earl of Clarendon, 75, 78; Lord Rochester, 78, 80; Lawrence, of Hatch, 69; Robert, of Dinton, 74

Iley Oak, 35
Imber, 113, 116, 118
Ine, King of Wessex, 30, 31, 33
Inglesham, 37, 101
Ivychurch Priory, 54, 65

James: I, 74; II, 78, 79, 83
Jane (Seymour), Queen, 60
Jewel, Bishop, 68
Julius Caesar, 23

Katherine, Queen, 63
Kennet & Avon Canal, 101, 102
Kennet Valley, 42, 62, 121
Kent, William, 90
Kilmington, 107
Kingswood (Glos.), 65, 66, 87

Kingston Deverill, 116
Kitson, John, 62
Knap Hill, 14
Knook, 37
Knoyle, East and West, 9, 39, 49, 112
Knyvett, Sir Henry, 69

Labourers, Statutes of, 55
Lacock Abbey and estate, 47, 49, 57, 64, 65, 66, 67, 69
Lake House, 70
Landsdowne, Marquess of (Petty-Fitzmaurice family), 100
Larkhill, 115
Laud, William, Archbishop, 68, 73, 74
Laverton, Abraham, 112
Lavington, Dauntsey's School, 83
Layton & Legh, Commissioners, 65
Leigh Delamere, 37
Levant Company, 87
Limpley Stoke, 119
Lisieux estate, 40, 41
Littlecote, 27, 70
Long: family, 62, 82, 111, 116; Edward, of Monkton Farleigh, 69; Richard, of Rood Ashton, 109; Robert, of Wraxall, 59; Walter, of Dauntsey, 73
Longbridge Deverill, 48, 57, 62, 85
Longford Castle, 70, 76, 77, 82, 90, 109
Longleat, 61, 63, 84, 86, 88, 90, 92, 109, 116, see also Thynne
Longespée, William, Earl of Salisbury, 51
Lucas, Walter, 59
Ludgershall, 41, 97
Ludlow: family, of Hill Deverill, 72; Edmund and Armada, 69; Edmund, regicide, 77
Lydiard Tregoze, 45, 55, 68, 88, 116
Lyneham airfield, 115

Macadam, J. L., 100
Maiden Bradley, 49, 65, 66, 107
Maiden Castle (Dorset), 24
Malet, Sir Henry, 113
Malmesbury, 33, 35, 36, 37, 39, 40, 43, 44, 46, 48, 49, 55, 57, 58, 62, 65, 66, 67, 76, 86, 88, 100, 106, 119, 122
Manningford Bruce, 48
Marden, 16, 17
Marlborough, 41, 44, 57, 62, 65, 66, 68, 74, 76, 77, 86, 88, 97, 100, 104, 118

Marlborough Downs, 14, 18, 115, 120, 121
Marston Meysey, 101
Marx, Karl, 88
Mary: Tudor, 61, 68, 73; II, 78
Matilda (or Maud), Empress of Germany, 46
Mauduit family, 47
Maynard, Alan, 69
Melchet Forest, 43
Melksham, 57, 71, 84, 88, 96, 98, 106, 119
Melksham Forest, 45, 73
Mere, 53, 57, 58, 118
Mervyn, Sir John, 69
Methuen: family, 62, 82, 112; John, 82
Mildenhall: Cunetio, 26; Hungerford estate, 57
Monkton Farleigh, 65, 66
Monmouth, Duke of, 78
Montacute (Somerset), 41
Montague, John, Earl of Salisbury, 59
Morgan's Hill, 31
Motorway (M4), 121

Neeld estate, 109
Nelson, Admiral Horatio, 90
Nennius, 30
Nestlé, 118
Netheravon, 37
Nettleton Shrub, temple at, 27
Nicholas of Ely, 52
North Wiltshire Canal, 101
Norton Bavant, 87

Oaksey, 41
Oakwood, 55
Odo (Bishop of Bayeux), 41
Ogbourne, 48, 63
Ogilby's Road Atlas (1675), 100
Osmund, Saint (Bishop of Salisbury), 67
Osney Abbey, Oxford, 63, 66
Overton, 16, 17, 41
Oxford University, 52, 76

Peasant's Revolt of 1381, 55
Pembroke, Earl of, 61, 69, 74, 82
Pembroke estate, 72, 92, 93, 109, 116, see also Wilton
Pembrokeshire stones, 17, 18
Penrudduck, Col., of Compton Chamberlayne, 77
Pepys, Samuel, 99
Pewsey: 98; Vale of, 31, 39, 42, 109
Pewsham Forest, 73
Philipps House (Dinton), 112
Pit Meads (Sutton Veny), 26

Pitt: Thomas, 81; William, Earl of Chatham, 82
Poor Law: Elizabethan, 70; New (1834), 70 and Chapter IX
Poore, Richard, Bishop of Salisbury, 51
Popham, Chief Justice, 70; & Littlecote Estate, 116
Poulton, 65, 66
Powell, Dr., Canon of Salisbury, 67
Purton, 57
Purton Stoke Spa, 88
Pythouse (Benett), 95, 112

Quemerford, 112
Quidhampton (Pembroke estate), 92

Radnor, Earls of (Bouverie family, of Longford), 109
Railways: Great Western, 103-6; London & South Western, 104; Wiltshire, Somerset & Weymouth, 104
Ramsbury, diocese and estate, 39, 44
Ravenhill, Thomas, 96
Reeves of Bratton, 119
Reform Act (1832), 82
Repton, Humphrey, 90
Richard: II, 55; III, 60
Ridgeway, 16, 17
Robin Hood's Ball, 14
Roger, Bishop of Salisbury, 46, 48
Rood Ashton (Long family), 116
Roundway, battle of (nr. Devizes), 176
Rowcombe (nr. Malmsbury), 55
Rybury, 14

St John family, of Lydiard, 68, 116
Salisbury: Earl of, 41, 47; New, 9, 50-53, 54, 57, 58, 60, 62, 63, 67, 73, 76, 78, 80, 81, 82, 83, 87, 95, 97, 98, 99, 100, 104, 105, 106, 109, 111, 113, 115, 118, 119, 120, 121, 122; Old (Searobyrig or Sarum), 9, 24, 26, 31, 35, 39, 41, 44, 46, 48, 50, 81, 99, 111; Plain, 91, 99, 113, 114, 120
Sanctuary, The, 16
Sandy Lane, 9, 26
Sarum, see Old Salisbury, 26
Savernake Forest, 31, 45, 60, 89, 109, 116
Scout Motors of Salisbury, 119
Scratchbury, 21
Seend, 59

127

Selwood Forest, 33, 35, 49, 73
Semington, 101
Semley, 105
Senior, Nassau, 96
Settlement, Act of (1662), 71
Seymour: family, 78, 82, 88, 111;
  Edward, Duke of Somerset,
  60, 61, 66, 68, 69; Francis,
  Earl of Trowbridge, 74; Jane,
  Queen of England, 60;
  William, Lord Hertford, later
  Duke of Somerset, 74
Shaftesbury Abbey Estate, 43
Shalbourne, 84
Sharington, William, 66, 67, 68
Shaxton, Bishop of Salisbury, 67-
  8
Shepton Mallet (Somerset), 87
Sherborne, 33, 35
Sherston, 41, 50
Silbury Hill, 16, 17, 24
Silchester (Hants), 24
Skimmington, Lady, 73
Smythe, John, 62
Smythson, Robert, 69
Snap, 116
Somerford, 41
Somerset: Dukes, see Seymour;
  estate, 109
Somerset House, 69, 96
Somerset Coal Canal, 101, 106
Southampton, 53, 62
South Newton, 87
Speenhamland (Berks.), 95
Spanish Armada (1588), 69
Standlynch church, 80
Stanley Abbey, 53, 65, 66
Staverton, 118
Steeple Ashton, 59, 87
Steeple Longford, 53
Stephen, King of England, 46, 47
Stockton, 23, 41, 70
Stokys, John, 59
Stonehenge, 9, 16, 17, 113, 115
Stourhead, 90, 109
Stourton, Lord, 60, 61
Stratford-sub-Castle, 53, 81
Stratton: 105; family, 109
Stumpe, William, 62, 66
Suffolk, Earls of (& Berkshire),
  88, 91, 109
Sutton Veny, 16, 26, 112
Sweyn, 36
Swindon, 50, 82, 104, 105, 106,
  108, 112, 113, 119, 121, 122
'Swing' riots, 93, 94, 96

Taylor, S. Watson, estate of, 109
Thames & Severn Canal, 101
Thames Valley, 23, 31
Thamesdown District, 122
Theodosius, Roman General, 27,
  28
Thynne family, of Longleat, 61,
  69, 74, 78, 83, 116, see also
  Bath, Weymouth and
  Longleat
Tidworth, 113, 115
Tilshead, 15, 35, 39, 43, 59
Tincommius, 23
Tisbury, 57, 95
Titt, Wallis, of Warminster, 119
Tollard Royal, 23
Topp, John, of Stockton, 70
Tottenham (Savernake), 89, 90,
  92, 112, 116
Touchet, James, Baron Audley,
  60
Tregoze family, 47
Tropenell family, 59
Trowbridge, 41, 46, 59, 74, 87,
  97, 100, 105, 106, 111, 118,
  119, 121
Tull, Jethro, 84

Upavon, 115
Upham, 170
Upton Lovell, 'Golden Barrow',
  19

Vastern: Park, 55; Estate, 109
Verica, 23
Verlucio (Sandy Lane), 26
Vespasian, General (later Roman
  Emperor), 24

Waller, General Sir William, 76
Wanborough, 26, 57
Wansdyke, 31, 36
Wansey family, of Warminster, 87
Warbeck, Perkin, 60
Wardour: (Old) Castle, 69, 70,
  76; New, 89; Vale of, 43
Warminster, 9, 5, 39, 43, 45, 50,
  57, 58, 74, 77, 83, 86, 87, 93,
  96, 98, 99, 104, 105, 106, 111,
  115, 121
West family, 31
West Dean, 26
West Kennet, 17
West Lavington, 57
West Overton, 16, 17, 26
Westbury, 58, 66, 104, 106, 112

Westwood, 59
Wexcombe, 116
Weymouth, Lord (Thynne of
  Longleat), 83
Whitesheet Hill, 14, 21
Wilcot, 41
Willoughby de Broke family, 60
William: I, 36, 38, 39, 45; II, 46;
  III (of Orange), 78, 79, 83
Wilmot, Henry, 76
Wilsaetan, 33
Wilton, 33, 35, 37, 39, 43, 46, 49,
  51, 52, 57, 58, 59, 61, 62, 65,
  66, 67, 76, 86, 95, 99, 106,
  109, 112, 116
Wilton House, 61, 69, 74, 80, 88,
  90
Wiltshire & Berkshire Canal,
  101, 104
Wiltshire Horned sheep, 71, 92
Wiltshire Regiment, 115
Wiltshire, Somerset & Weymouth
  Railway, 104
Winchcombe, Jack, of Newbury,
  62
Winchester: 31, 51, 53, 100;
  Bishop of, estates, 39, 47, 49,
  50, 54, 57
Windmill Hill, 14
Winterbourne Bassett, 16
Winterbourne Stoke, 17, 120
Winterslow, 95
Wither, Anthony, 73
Wolf Hall (nr. Bedwyn), 60, 80,
  89
Wolsey, Thomas, Cardinal, 63
Wood, John, the elder, 84
Woodbury, 23
Woodhenge, 16
Wootton Bassett, 50, 101, 104,
  105
Wraxall, 59
Wren, Christopher, 9
Wroughton, Sir Thomas, 69
Wyatt: Matthew Digby, 112;
  T.H., 112
Wylie: 101; people of, 38; River,
  38; valley, 21, 22, 38, 54, 71,
  93
Wyndham family, 112

Yarnbury, 21
Yerbury family, 62

Zeals airfield, 115